ENOUGH
TO MAKE YOU
BLUSH

EXPLORING EROTIC HUMILIATION

UPDATED EDITION

BY PRINCESS KALI

AN EROTICATION PUBLICATION

Other Books by Princess Kali

Enough to Make You Blush: Companion Workbook

Behind the Blush: Humiliation Confessions: Volume 1 & 2

Making Bank: A Money Management Workbook for Erotic Entrepreneurs

The Yes, No, Maybe Workbook: Get What you Want Out of Sex & Kink

365 Days of Kink: A Journal of Sex Self Discovery

Scene Notes: Plan & Reflect On Your Kink Adventures

Authentic Kink: Create Your Best Experience

Forthcoming Titles

ProDomme Playbook

This book is dedicated to sexual adventurers and erotic rebels. You never cease to inspire me.

TABLE OF CONTENTS

Ways to Play

FOREWORD

I PUBLISHED THE FIRST EDITION of this book in 2015, but even then, it had been a long time coming. In the first year of my career as an educator, I attended a class taught by Jay Wiseman (author of the popular book *SM 101: A Realistic Introduction*). I went up to him afterward and thanked him for his influential BDSM books, and he said, "Oh yes, Princess Kali! I've heard you're the go-to girl for humiliation."

I had been teaching humiliation classes for several months, and I was proud my name had already traveled so successfully around the community. I decided right then and there that I would embrace the title of "go-to girl for humil-iation" by writing the seminal book on the subject. After all, it was my kinky passion, and there was a huge dearth of resources out there on the subject. Why shouldn't I be the one to fill the void? So, I spent the next decade or so creating systems, collecting insights, and putting my ideas together.

A few years after I first met him, I had lunch with Jay, who had by then become a friend and Kink Academy colleague, and told him about the book I'd been slowly working on ever since that fateful day. He enthusiastically encouraged me to finish, and that was all the nudge I needed. I ran with it from there, and since I published the first edition, it has been so validating to see it take off in the kink community. *Enough to Make You Blush* has sold more than ten thousand copies, and I have heard from countless readers who've expressed their gratitude, not only for the information I shared in the book, but for the way the book made them feel seen and understood—often for the very first time. I have been incredibly honored by this response over the years, and I'm thrilled to have solidified my standing as the "go-to girl for humiliation" as *Enough to Make You Blush* has helped me transform my passion into a driving purpose.

Why release an updated edition seven years later? It's almost incomprehensible to me that seven years have passed since I published the first edition of this book; it feels like both an eternity and an instant. But in those seven years, I've learned more, and having seen the impact this book has already had on so many people, I know that I owe it to my community to continue sharing knowledge, insights, and ideas. The concepts in the first edition of *Enough to Make You Blush* were—and still are—incredibly important and useful for both new and veteran kinsters. And yet, after I published the book and my reputation continued to grow along with it, I had the opportunity to teach even more humiliation classes, present at even more conferences, and learn from even more players about their experiences. During all that time, although erotic humiliation has gained more acceptance in the kink world, *Enough to Make You Blush* has remained the only major resource on the subject. So, with distinct pleasure, I've embraced the responsibility of expanding the conversation by refining my material on what I've learned.

So, what's changed between the first edition and this one?

First and foremost, I've conducted a new survey, which, combined with the responses to my original *Enough to Make*

You Blush survey, gives me (and by extension you) access to insights and anecdotes from 1,139 people about their experiences with erotic humiliation. As a result, I've been able to add even more unique and diverse perspectives to this edition than there were in the first (and there were *a lot* in the first). You'll see those in the quotes that accompany each chapter, adding a layer of depth to the book that I, as just one person with just one set of experiences, could not create on my own.

Next, like before, the first part of the book provides a holistic overview of erotic humiliation—what it is, why we like it, and how to do it in a safe, emotionally thoughtful way. But in this new edition, I've expanded on some critical concepts that, seven years ago, I didn't explore deeply enough. You'll learn more about what it means to find your kernel kink than you learned in the previous edition, and you'll see an expanded discussion of the complicated cultural contexts that make erotic humiliation possible in the first place. You'll also see a brand new chapter that takes an in-depth look at the ethics of this kind of play.

Also like before, the second half of the book explores more tactical, practical ideas for bringing your humiliation fantasies to life, and you'll find some fun new concepts in this edition, including a brand new chapter on impact play.

I'm proud to present you with the second edition of *Enough to Make You Blush.* I hope that, whether you've already read the first edition or you're meeting this text for the first time, whether you're a veteran humiliation player or just beginning to explore this desire, these pages will give you the information, inspiration, and confidence you need to bring your erotic fantasies to life.

INTRODUCTION

EROTIC HUMILIATION IS a complex, varied, and mostly misunderstood fetish. It isn't just about smeared mascara and groveling under boots; it's also about exploring vulnerability, trust, control, and sacrifice through absurdity, amusement, and consensual cruelty. Yet, all the stereotypes and misconceptions can create apprehension about trying this intensely psychological kind of play, even for those who have a deep desire to experience it.

If you've ever looked for guidance on playing with erotic humiliation, you've likely discovered that there are not many resources available on the subject. There are plenty of books and videos available about rope bondage or dominance and submission, but few with a focus on psychological play. I've heard many kinksters express frustration with the lack of information available. This book is intended to fix that.

Enough to Make You Blush will equip both light and heavy players with exciting new ideas to use and expand upon. Do you know you're interested but haven't figured anything out beyond that? Have you played with embarrassment or humiliation but want to improve your play? Are you a "hardcore" player ready to play deeper and/or wider? Regardless of where you are on the spectrum of experience, this book will inspire insights and arouse a new level of creativity in your play!

WHO AM I?

My name is Princess Kali, and I was a professional dominatrix based in Boston, Massachusetts, for over twelve years. I've also been a lifestyle dominant for twenty-one years and counting, and I'm a dedicated sex and kink educator. I have always had a dominant and rather big personality, so when I discovered the kink scene, I jumped in with both feet!

That is, I used my feet to jump at the opportunity to model at a foot fetish party in New York City. I was twenty-two and up for a sexy adventure, having no idea that it would lead me to an as-yet-unmatched passion and mission in my life.

Since that fateful first foot fetish party, I have hosted my own foot fetish parties through Footnight™ events, owned six commercial dungeons, sessioned with hundreds of individuals, and starred in and managed a successful female domination pornography website including thirty-two self-produced DVDs. As an educator, I launched the revolutionary video-based sex education website KinkAcademy.com in 2007 (soon to be followed by the more vanilla website PassionateU.com). I have taught over 250 classes at more than 65 different events and organizations, both kinky and mainstream. In 2020, I launched Red Key Club, a business and marketing school and community for sex workers, and in 2022 I was inducted into the Dominatrix Hall of Fame. This book was the start of a love of self-publishing, and since its original publication I've added another eleven book and workbook titles including *Authentic Kink* and the *Yes, No, Maybe Workbook*.

After more than twenty years, it's safe to say that I've lived a life of "full-immersion perversion" and continue to discover new ways that I want to help others feel empowered, informed, and inspired in their own lives.

Despite my wealth of experience, however, the fact is that I am a white, cisgendered, queer female whose experience has mostly centered around heterosexual interactions with cisgendered submissive men. The main voice of this book is my own and speaks from my personal experiences. I believe my experiences are adaptable, and I've included a wide variety of voices to capture other experiences as well, but I want to disclose my position and privileges upfront.

WHAT THIS BOOK ISN'T

First and foremost, *Enough to Make You Blush* is not a therapist endorsement of any of the activities discussed within these chapters, or of your particular experiences, as healthy or unhealthy.

BDSM, and erotic humiliation play in particular, are so personal that there's no absolute way to determine if what you're experiencing is "healthy" (which is a subjective concept anyway). There are risks, but there are risks in almost all kink (and life), and only you can determine whether they're risks you're comfortable with and willing to take. Just like with all other kinks, you can play with emotional masochism at the level that's comfortable/erotic for you, and while this book will give you insight into what that might look like, it *cannot* prescribe specific activities or levels that are "right" for you.

Additionally, this book makes no judgments as to your particular fantasies. The wonderful thing about BDSM and your fantasies is that they are exactly that—*your* fantasies. No one can tell you they're right or wrong, as long as everyone is getting what they need as safely as possible and no one is getting hurt without their consent.

Next, this book is not an attempt to make erotic humiliation "make sense." Because, no matter how experienced you are with this kind of play, the reality is that it doesn't always "make sense." In fact, it often makes *no* sense. And that's okay. Sexuality is extremely complex, and we barely have language to describe the more traditional sexual interests, let alone the psychologically entangled and unusual ones. But that doesn't matter. In my opinion, there are three fundamental basics that should be met to determine if what you're doing is "good" for you:

1. You are giving your informed and uncoerced consent, and so is your partner. This is paramount.

2. It turns you on. Engaging in it is exciting, arousing, and/or sexually satisfying.

3. You are ultimately glad you did it.

We'll explore these consent points more deeply throughout the book, but it's important to establish them upfront so you can keep them in mind as you read—and as you play.

Kink has a lot of depths to explore, both within yourself and in others. But that shouldn't be taken on lightly, especially with humiliation. We do *not* want to damage each other in any real or permanent way. Ultimately, kink and humiliation should be a positive experience for everyone involved. If it's not, then it's time to rethink it.

> *There is nothing better for mental health around kink than being able to share it with a positive community.*
> *—All These Roadworks*

Finally, this book is also not intended as an exhaustive list of humiliating activities or an exhaustive encyclopedia of everything you could ever imagine related to erotic humiliation. Don't get me wrong—it's *quite* comprehensive, and I'm confident it will provide a wide range of novel and thought-provoking ideas to new and veteran players alike; but as you'll read, so much of humiliation has to do with the individual players' mindset and psychology that it's impossible to list every single thing that a person might find erotically humiliating. Both parts of this book—the theory and guidance in the first half and the activity chapters in the second—are meant to inspire self-reflection, encourage conversations with partners, and provide fodder for a "starter list" of actions you might consider when planning a scene.

WHAT THIS BOOK IS

This book is one woman's perspective (albeit a highly educated and experienced perspective) on erotic humiliation, enriched by the voices of the larger kink community.

I'm writing this book with a goal of offering concrete ideas. Based on my years of experiences, these suggestions will make, at the very least, an excellent jumping off point for your own fantasies. I will be honest when I think a fantasy should stay just that, and I will give you tips on making some of the edgier ones happen realistically and safely. But again, ultimately, you are an adult and have to make your own decisions.

The main instruction in this book tends to slightly favor dominant roles, as that's where my experience is and that's the side that tends to be responsible for planning sessions. However, I've included plenty of tips, strategies and insights for submissives as well, along with a lot of submissive perspectives pulled from survey responses. (So if you're a switch you get double the awesome!) As I always say, "Kink is a team sport, so everyone needs to get in the game!"

While many of the ideas in this book can stand alone to make for exciting play, you should also feel free to mix and match, and you'll see some overlap of tactics from chapter to chapter. I leave it to you to create the matrix of experiences that is best for your desires. Additionally, because humiliation is such a varied interest, I'll never be able to get to everything in this book. (If I tried, this thing would weigh twenty pounds!) So, I encourage you to add additional activities and fantasies to your play.

As I've mentioned, you'll also see that I've included ideas and quotes from other kinksters and educators throughout this book. These are the fruits of a survey I sent out about erotic humiliation, once in 2014 and 2015 and again in three different iterations during 2021 and 2022, with a combined 1,139 responses. Because humiliation play takes place in the mind, I figured the more minds the merrier!

A note about the quotes: They were all collected and shared consensually from survey responses and have been edited only lightly for greater ease of reading. It was important to me to highlight voices other than my own, so as much as possible, I preserved respondents' language, style, and punctuation. All names are listed as respondents requested, including many that are anonymous or represented by a letter (either because they indicated they wanted to be anonymous or because they consented to being quoted but didn't list a pseudonym).

HOW TO USE THIS BOOK

My recommendation is that you start at the beginning and read straight through. The early information regarding safety, communication, ethics, and the process of setting up a healthy experience is crucial to being able to put the activities I recommend in the second half to good use. If you feel like you simply have to jump ahead, then go take a peek at the activities chapters, but before you put anything into play, come back and read the other stuff. Believe me: when you use the detailed information and guidance from the first half of the book to create more successful experiences with the "fun stuff," you'll be glad you took the time.

Whether you're coupled and can put these ideas into action immediately or you're single and trying to learn more about your needs for the future, this book can be a source of inspiration as well as instruction to fulfilling your kinky desires.

As you come across intriguing concepts and unfamiliar terms, I encourage you to use this book as a springboard for further research and learning. To get you started, I've included an extensive resource list, as well as a glossary. (Throughout the text, certain words and terms will be **bolded** to indicate that they're included in the glossary.)

Before we get started, let me provide a quick (but important) reminder that this book assumes that you are a legal adult engaging in consensual and erotically intentioned kinky play with another legal adult. You assume responsibility for your own physical and psychological safety. I accept no liability for your actions or their results.

CHAPTER 1

WHAT IS EROTIC HUMILIATION?

Here's the thing, anything can be humiliating with the right people and the right context. What may be innocent and sweet to me may be devastatingly humiliating to you.

- Kk

FIRST THINGS FIRST. WHAT IS humiliation? One of the most important things to remember when it comes to this type of play is that everyone's experience is going to be vastly different. There is no such thing as a universally "humiliating activity," because what one person finds degrading another person might find liberating. What constitutes humiliation entirely depends on the mindsets of the people involved. So there's no perfect formula—it really is something you have to personalize. But we can get on the same page about the general concept of humiliation. Here's how the American Psychological Association defines it:

A feeling of shame as a result of being disgraced or deprecated. The feeling sometimes leads to severe depression and deterioration of the individual's sense of self-esteem. Humiliation of a partner is frequently found in relationships characterized by sexual sadism and sexual masochism.

Now, while it's a start, I take issue with the APA definition, and here's why: Humiliation play, done responsibly, should never lead "to severe depression and deterioration of the individual's self-esteem." These negative consequences are the result of *shame*, which is related to but different from *humiliation*. Shame, in our everyday lives, is about our perceptions of the way other people perceive us—it's all about the fear that people are thinking poorly of you because you're doing, thinking, or feeling something that deviates from what you're *supposed* to be doing, thinking, or feeling. Humiliation, on the other hand, in the context of play, is about purposely pursuing that misalignment between what we're "supposed" to do and what we want to do or are doing—and then making it feel good. (More on this in chapter 2, when we discuss cultural context.) The APA definition's blunt approach misses that nuance between shame and humiliation. They're related concepts, and humiliation can only exist in play because shame exists outside of it, but the results couldn't be more different.

Erotic humiliation is about taking a "real world" thing/word/action that a player understands as "humiliating" (whether it's commonly understood as such or not) and re-contextualizing it as erotic play by adding a layer of acceptance, appreciation, and mutual enjoyment that converts what "should" be a shameful experience into an enjoyable one. I like to call this "The Pervert Paradox" ("pervert" being a former slur that I've reclaimed as unequivocally positive) because it explores such contradictory feelings of desiring to do all these things we've been taught to avoid, or even abhor. Contradiction of society and feeling. The result is that players reclaim these traditionally negative experiences such as guilt, shame, and disgrace, and use them to create attraction and arousal during **consensual** interactions.

Although humiliation looks different to everybody, it's important to understand how the real world context we all share forms the basis for why the activities used in play are humiliating. I'll explore this in depth in the next chapter, but for now, here's what you need to know: Erotic humiliation plays on concepts like misogyny, gender roles, classism, and other cultural contexts that generally illicit the "ick factor" to create an experience that is ultimately pleasurable, rather than offensive, injurious, or disgusting.

It is entirely possible to make just about any activity a humiliating one, depending on the desire of the bottom to participate. Taking away their control of the situation and forcing them to do something unsavory or embarrassing to them is the very nature of humiliation. So if they are embarrassed by their desire to sleep with a woman, to eat oatmeal or to watch network television, these can all be humiliating tasks. And eroticism is simply introducing an element of the erotic into that situation. So maybe giving him a handjob while he is forced to watch American Idol could in fact be humiliating. Period.

- Mr Ogre

Social hierarchies are an essential part of any civilization; they are also an integral part of our individual identities. To a large extent, we define ourselves by our positions in these hierarchies. It's important to our egos to know just how high up on the social ladder we are—and equally important to believe that we belong there. When something happens that shows us that we don't belong there—or when something happens (i.e., when we do something) that moves us down the ladder, we feel embarrassment or shame. Otherwise known as humiliation. In erotic play, these traditionally negative feelings are connected with arousal.

What really makes an activity humiliating—erotically or not—is the knowledge that somebody else has seen it or knows about it. For example, tripping and falling hurts no matter what, but it's only embarrassing when someone else sees it or you have to tell someone about it. And the same is true in erotic humiliation. In fact, one thing that has come up in many of my workshops is the need for an act to be witnessed by at least one other person for it to be humiliating. The simple idea that someone—even just your long-term partner—is witnessing the "weird" or "terrible" or "awful" thing you're doing is an important part of the psychology of humiliation, because *that*—and not the activity itself—is what creates the feelings of shame. (Note that this idea is separate from public play or exhibitionism, though we'll get into that later.)

IS EROTIC HUMILIATION A FETISH OR A KINK?

The short answer to this question is, "It depends." More specifically, it depends on whether humiliation is a "must have" or a "nice to have" for a particular player.

Lately, the word **fetish** has been used flexibly to cover a wide range of sexual preferences, but if we're getting technical, a fetish is a form of sexual desire in which gratification is linked *to an abnormal degree* to a particular object, item of clothing, part of the body, etc. This means that, if an individual has a humiliation *fetish*, then humiliation *must* be part of the sexual process in order for them to climax (or even become aroused in the first place).

Humiliation is certainly a fetish for some, but it's more commonly a **kink**, which refers to a strong sexual attraction to nontraditional interests. A kink is a taste or a preference, but it's a "nice to have," not a "must have."

More often than not, "kink" is a more accurate description than "fetish" when we're talking about people who enjoy erotic humiliation. This is often just one of many interests in the BDSM realm.

It's one of my many kinks. It doesn't define me or my sex life, but it can be an intense addition.

- RL

STEREOTYPES ABOUT EROTIC HUMILIATION

A lot of folks who might be curious about erotic humiliation avoid exploring it because, more than just about any other aspect of **BDSM**, it's tied up in a long list of negative stereotypes about both the behavior and the people who engage in it. If these stereotypes have stopped you from exploring your interests and desires, you're not alone. My goal now is to help you reframe your thinking so they're no longer an obstacle in the way of your fantasies. There are a lot of myths and stereotypes surrounding humiliation play, so let's look at three of the most common ones.

ONLY DAMAGED PEOPLE LIKE IT

People on both sides of the humiliation dynamic worry about what their desire for this kind of play says about them. I'll speak more extensively later in the book about why people like it, but for now I want to address two corollary ideas: first, that only people with low confidence and low self-worth would let someone humiliate them, and second, that those who want to humiliate are hateful and genuinely disgusted by their partners.

My experience and research show that neither is true. Nearly 70 percent of people who responded to my survey said they thoroughly enjoy their desire for erotic humiliation play and feel that a high level of confidence is an important part of engaging in healthy erotic humiliation. Others noted that, although they are very confident already, erotic humiliation is actually an opportunity to recreate an "emotional ordeal" that allows them to look their insecurities right in the face, and the result is that they come out on the other side feeling even stronger and more sure of themselves.

The biggest concern most respondents expressed was judgment from others in cases of nonconsensual discovery. My experiences support that finding, as well. I'd estimate that 90 percent of the submissives I've played with have very high self-esteem. In fact, I've found that the people I've played with tend to think very highly of themselves. Perhaps that's part of why they are so turned on by being humiliated.

The humiliation for me does not come from a lack of confidence or self-esteem, but from the interplay between knowing I am strong, smart, capable, and knowing I get turned on from being told I am none of those things and less.

- Em the Sissy

IT'S ABUSIVE

Even within the larger kink community, there seems to be an attitude that there is more potential for abuse with psychological play than physical play, but that's not entirely true. No, psychological play won't leave any bruises for others to see, but safety is safety, and when partners engage in consensual humiliation play, even when they're pushing boundaries, they are doing so for the purpose of pleasure while keeping each others' safety in focus. I'll talk in detail about the line between humiliation and abuse in chapter 3, but for now, just know that, when players are building on a foundation of trust and consent, erotic humiliation is not abusive.

For a long time I wouldn't let myself humiliate others because I don't enjoy experiencing humiliation myself. I had to realize they are having a very different experience than I am. I just feel emotional pain. They feel much more and experience much more.

- S

IT'S CRUEL

Another really common myth that hinders people from exploring erotic humiliation is the idea that it's cruel, and that submissives are supposed to feel "bad." For those who aren't attracted to this kind of play, it can seem outright repulsive (which can be the appeal for a certain type of humiliation player). So, trying to wrap their heads around the psychological and emotional version of "pleasurable pain" can be difficult. Here's the key distinction: Cruelty is born of sudden and inexplicably intense action, whereas consensual humiliation is nuanced and exists within well-established boundaries.

To play well and safely at any intensity level takes a very strong level of affection between the people in the **scene**. This affection, combined with frequent check-ins using established language or signals, ensures that nobody ever has to exceed their own limits. (Of course, that doesn't mean they're not then humiliated for their incompetence and reticence!)

There are other [activities] I simply wouldn't do because I find them too hurtful, like body image insults, or calling him a loser. Anything I do that involves humiliation play really must at its core be something that binds us or helps the two of us bond. I would never want to do anything that does any actual psychological harm, or even makes him doubt my love.

- Anonymous

And by the way, sometimes erotic humiliation is exactly the opposite of cruel. **Praise kink** has been trending lately, and as a fan and frequent perpetrator of aggressive pep talks, I am here for it. Here's how it works: The dominant requires the submissive to stand in front of them and receive sincere compliments until they're so overwhelmed and embarrassed they can't stand it. Why does this work? Because for most people, accepting compliments without downplaying our achievements or positive traits is incredibly difficult and embarrassing. So the goal of praise kink, far from cruelty or degradation, is to embarrass a willing sub into oblivion by telling them incredibly true and complimentary things about themselves. It's a surprising, beautiful, and healthy form of erotic humiliation and a great example of how this kind of play is diverse and has the potential for a wide range of emotional experiences and intents.

OTHER STEREOTYPES AND MISCONCEPTIONS

The stereotypes listed above are the most common, but they certainly aren't the only ones out there. Others that have come up in my workshops include the following:

- "It's all about being brutal."
- "That it's disrespectful.
- "People assume it's nonconsensual."
- "That you're not right in the head."
- "It's a dysfunctional way to play."
- "There's no way for it to be spiritual."
- "That there is no connection between players."
- "The humiliator is insecure, so therefore, they must be mean to others."
- "That people engage in this *only* to relive past trauma."
- "The dominant is seen as being careless."
- "That it's exploitative."
- "It's payback for past experiences."

These assumptions (and many more) might come from other kink players, or we might struggle with them ourselves. It can be helpful to consider what stereotypes we might be internalizing in order to overcome those obstacles and achieve the most pleasurable, healthy expression of erotic humiliation.

INTENSITY

People tend to think of humiliation play as a very one-level, one-volume activity. (The image that likely comes to mind is one of a leather-clad dom(me) yelling, "Go lick my toilet, you maggot!") Sure, that's one style, but like everything in BDSM, there are multiple ways to play. One of my favorite things about teaching erotic humiliation is seeing audience members realize that they are already incorporating this type of energy into their scenes. When you broaden your understanding of what erotic humiliation *is*, you might be surprised at what you're attracted to! From light embarrassment to full-on cruelty and degradation, this kind of play exists on a spectrum, and its **intensity** is based on the differential we talked about before, between how you're "supposed" to act and how you want to or are acting. The further you stray from "normal" or "acceptable" in your play, the higher the intensity. In general, we can break humiliation play into three levels of intensity, which can be increased through words, actions, or a combination of the two.

EMBARRASSMENT

To embarrass someone is to cause them to experience a state of self-conscious distress. Embarrassment is fairly low-level play, along the lines of teasing or even flirting. The physical equivalent of this kind of humiliation might be a pinch on the cheek. It may be annoying, and you can certainly feel it, but it's not going to do any real damage or startle you too much. Embarrassments are usually simple things that might happen to anyone, but they become embarrassing when attention is called to them.

> As an example, I like to use the idea of a submissive accidently walking out of the bathroom with toilet paper stuck on the bottom of their shoe in a public place. If you are engaged in embarrassment play, you might lean close and whisper in their ear, "Jeez, everybody's going to notice that filthy toilet paper on your filthy slut shoes." Or a bit more intense might be instructing them, "You have to walk around for another two minutes with that toilet paper on your shoe." This level involves subtle, more playful kinds of teasing, which is mostly kept between the two players.

HUMILIATION

The next level is true humiliation. To humiliate someone is to reduce them to a lower position in their own eyes or the eyes of others by showing disdain and/or engaging in harsher and more intense behaviors.

This is the middle level of intensity, and in terms of a physical action, you can liken it to a face slap. It's less playful than that pinch on the cheek, and it's got an edge to it. If you're the one doing the humiliating, you're delivering more of a blow, but you're not knocking them out.

Returning to the toilet paper, you might say out loud to other people, "Look at this filthy slut! Can't even get the toilet paper off their shoe before they leave the bathroom." There's a slightly wider engagement, and perhaps it's a little more "mean-spirited."

DEGRADATION

To degrade somebody is to bring them to low esteem, and I mean hardcore. Degradation happens when a dominant takes a submissive to very low places.

This is the highest intensity of psychological play. It's savage, vicious, and can even be downright cruel. It's the right hook to the jaw, TKO, knocked the fuck out!

Back to the toilet paper example, you might loudly chastise, "You filthy whore, get in there and lick that toilet and then swallow that toilet paper."

"Can you even wipe your ass correctly? Everybody is going to be in here thinking that your stinky ass is on that toilet paper while you're dragging it around! Get down there and swallow that toilet paper. Suck it down!"

Degradation is where the real edge lives, and it requires the most trust and careful expertise to employ without causing unintended harm.

In case those stereotypes about abuse and cruelty are creeping back into your head as you read about degradation, let me remind you that humiliation play also involves mutual enjoyment and the commitment to lifting a partner back up after taking them down. The kind of cruelty that comes with degradation is consensual and takes place within carefully negotiated boundaries. Again, we'll talk more about this in chapter 3, but these activities take on a very different (abusive) edge when you are genuinely trying to nonconsensually break someone with no intention of giving them any sort of support afterward.

> *For a time I was in a verbally abusive relationship where the Dom essentially told me that the way he was talking to me wasn't abuse, it was part of our degradation play, and if I couldn't take it then I wasn't a real submissive. That relationship and some of the things he said had a really profound effect on my self esteem, and for several years I wasn't able to engage in any type of humiliation for fear of being triggered.*
>
> *- Anonymous*

Every intensity level can be applied to any kind of scene. Public play, objectification, service play, etc. can all range from mildly embarrassing to wildly degrading based on what both partners have agreed to beforehand. Just remember that, like when we're playing with physical pain, emotional pain comes in "good" and "bad" varieties, and it's our job to stay within the realm of "good" pain. Just because someone is caning their partner in a BDSM scene, that doesn't mean they have the right (or expectation) to punch them in the face. And the same is true in erotic humiliation. No emotional face punching, please.

STYLES OF HUMILIATION

It's not just the intensity of the humiliation that can vary, but the style as well. Four example styles of humiliation are sensual, authoritative, mocking, and cruel, and they can each look very different based on what level of play you're at. Let's take a look at each style, and see how it might be influenced by varied intensity levels.

SENSUAL

Psychological torment doesn't have to be severe, in fact, sensual embarrassment play is much more common than heavier degradation. With a sensual approach, the teasing is often focused on the submissive being aroused, with more overtly sexual tones, more physical intimacy, and a softer delivery.

For example: While out in public, a dominant might privately whisper a description of what their submissive looked like in a sexually compromising situation the night before, while "accidentally" brushing their nipples, to remind them of the feeling of exposure and to get them hot and bothered in an awkward situation. Does everyone know what a slut they are? Maybe! And that's quite exciting!

AUTHORITATIVE

This style is more about authority, with a strict and correctional tone. Being under someone's else's control can be infantilizing (even if you're not engaging in age play). Generally, the dominant in this style of play takes on the role of a "benevolent dictator," doling out punishments "for your own good."

For example: After delivering a belittling lecture about the dangers of chronic masturbation to a submissive with their underwear around their ankles, a dominant might put them over their knee for a spanking before standing them in the corner to think about how naughty they've been.

MOCKING

This classic style is all about robbing the submissive of their dignity. It brings to mind the schoolyard bully, using disdainful taunts and foolish predicaments to keep their target feeling off balance.

For example: After using a marker to write sexually derogatory comments all over their body, the dominant might command their submissive to have sex with a blow-up doll or to dress up in something ridiculous.

CRUEL

This is the most stereotypical style of play, but it's actually much less common. By its very nature, it will be more extreme than other styles, and it can have the appearance of real viciousness.

For example: A disdainful dominant might punish their submissive for minor protocol infraction by spitting in their face, using deeply derogatory language, and then putting their face in the toilet for a "swirly."

By playing with intensity and style, we can broaden the idea of humiliation so that even if you're not into "traditional" humiliation, you can still find some part of this psychological pool that you can play in. If you're working more with low-level embarrassment, then the style might be more playful and mocking. Humiliation and mid-level play likely has a stricter edge to it, with a dash of disgust. Degradation can be emphasized with a coldhearted demeanor, completely disgusted.

Recognize that you don't have to (and probably shouldn't) leap into the deep end of heavy humiliation, just like anything else in the kink world, but there's fun to be had in the shallows and infinite opportunity to wade deeper.

In short, humiliation requires that you tune in to the individual person that you're playing with. There's so much of the mind to explore, and people have such different approaches to desire that your ability to "poke at" all of those dark spaces is actually what makes humiliation play an exciting adventure. You're looking to combine intensity, style, limitations, interests, and actions to find humiliation that turns you on. It's an erotic Rubik's Cube!

CHAPTER 2

WHY DO PEOPLE ENJOY HUMILIATION?

Some activities can be both loved and hated. In fact the hating of the activity is what makes you love it.

- Anonymous

IF GROWING UP WATCHING *America's Funniest Home Videos* and the *Jackass* franchise taught us anything, it's that we like to laugh at other people's pain (*schadenfreude* is real). Many people are naturally sadistic in some way or another; most of us want to either suffer or dish out suffering.

For people with kinky desires, it makes perfect sense to want to be tied up. It is perfectly normal to want a spanking. However, the desire for erotic embarrassment doesn't "make sense" to many folks, even some of the kinksters who've been part of **The Scene** for a long time and who find physically focused play perfectly natural. But ultimately, the desire for humiliation comes from a very similar place as the desire for physical pain. Spoiler alert: taboo is really what BDSM is about. More than the actions of flogging or sploshing or crushing testicles under your feet, what we fundamentally do is play with taboo. That's what gives us the rush. It's about forbidden and transgressive behaviors. It's about doing things that not everybody does.

And yet, one thing that fascinates me about humiliation is just how deeply misunderstood it is. Not only are we not taught to love in this way, but on the surface it can look like we're doing the opposite of what a conventionally loving partner should do. Even among experienced kinksters, it's considered completely fine to whip somebody until they bleed, but emotional pain is completely unacceptable. Even people who love and enjoy really hardcore beatings or grueling intense bondage tell me, "I would never do that fucked-up humiliation stuff." There's very real judgment, even within the kink community. Why, they ask, would someone want to be knocked down a peg or two from off a perfectly good social hierarchy? That's what we're going to explore in this chapter.

WHERE DOES THIS KINK COME FROM?

There's no one answer to why people are interested in any particular kink, and the same is true for erotic humiliation. But there are several potential motivators—at both societal and individual levels—that could plant the seed for someone to enjoy humiliation play.

CULTURAL CONTEXT

Before we talk about the various reasons individuals might be attracted to erotic humiliation, let's talk about the phenomenon that makes it possible for erotic humiliation as a concept to even exist: cultural context.

Without cultural context there would be no erotic humiliation play. This is because it is the cultural context itself that teaches us—directly or subliminally—to be ashamed of or humiliated by certain things. We've been taught that straying from traditional gender roles makes us "deviant," that sleeping with too many people makes us "sluts." That making a living doing manual labor as opposed to white-collar desk jobs makes us somehow less than. Now, you and I may recognize that these societal "rules" and understandings are bogus, but the reality is that, without them, there would be nothing for anyone to be ashamed of—and no reason to flip that shame on its head and turn it into arousing, kinky play.

> *If there was no ego, there would be nothing to belittle, reduce, or attack. My erotic humiliation experiences have provided a wonderful counterbalance to my ego. This has helped me view ego more as a tool to deal with certain aspects of life than as a pillar of my identity. That kind of flexibility has ironically given me more confidence.*
>
> *- Anonymous*

Think of it as an iceberg. We can see about 10 percent of the iceberg's contents above the water—that's the arousal, embarrassment, fear, eroticism, shame, or guilt we're feeling as we engage in humiliation play. But underneath that, the other 90 percent of the iceberg is what really gives it substance and makes it powerful. That 90 percent below the surface includes all the cultural context, from gender stereotypes to fatphobia and body image expectations to transphobia and sexual morals to all the "isms"—sexism, classism, racism, ableism, and more. In everyday life, we may be fighting to eliminate these culturally ingrained expectations; in humiliation play, we're embracing them, turning them from negative stereotypes to opportunities for arousal.

CATALYST EXPERIENCES

Not only are we absorbing all of this cultural context from the world around us, but we may also have a specific experience in our youth that creates a developmental connection between embarrassment and arousal. This isn't true for everyone—only 34 percent of respondents to my recent surveys said they have an "origin story" of a particular experience inspiring their kink—in fact, lots of players simply encounter and come to enjoy erotic humiliation as adults. I've also found it more frequently true for submissives to have a specific catalyst for their kink, but it's possible for dominants to have a pivotal experience as well.

So, what does a catalyst experience look like?

For some people, it comes from a negative—even abusive—experience with authority figures who judged or punished them for sexual exploration when they were younger. For example, if someone was caught masturbating and severely punished for it, they may have learned later in life to short-circuit the "typical" responses to that experience (shame, reluctance to masturbate, avoidance of pleasure) and converted it into a source of erotic pleasure. For others, the negative experience was real-life humiliation by a lover or parter, such as blatant cheating or sexual rejection, which they then transmuted into a source of arousal as a way to cope.

But more often, the catalyst event is a peer-to-peer scenario of what I like to cheekily call "bullying that went well." They're teased or bullied, often but not always in a sexual way, but their brains' response is unexpected. Instead of, "Oh my God I never want that to happen to me again," their reaction is more along the lines of, "Oh my God, that was amazing! And there actually becomes a connection between the bullying activity and sexual satisfaction instead of mortification.

Back in school, I somehow became friends with a majority of the cheerleaders because I had sent a pic of myself shoving a marker in my ass. Frequently after that, I'd be invited to their house or on video call with the group asking me to and watching me masturbate for them, laughing and saying humiliating things to me. Ever since that day, I've had a core humiliation and small penis humiliation fetish.

- Connor D.

DEVELOPMENTAL CONTEXT

There is no escaping the larger context of the humiliating experiences or phrases we incorporate into our play, but as we just saw, a lot of how we perceive that context is filtered down from the broader culture through our own communities and personal experiences.

Think of it as a set of three concentric circles. The outermost circle is the messaging you're hearing from society as a whole, the next is your personal experiences, including what the communities you are part of (now or when you were younger) are telling you, and the innermost circle is how all those messages and experiences have filtered down to create your personal kinks and fetishes.

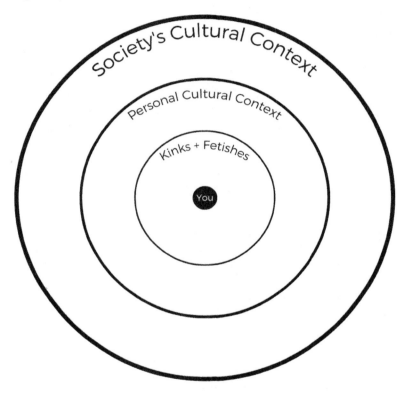

Let's zoom way out and use general attitudes toward sex as an example. (We could have this same conversation about racism, ageism, homophobia or any other ism, phobia, or prejudice you can think of.) In the outermost circle—society as a whole—you're hearing that women who have too much sex are sluts, that men who have a lot of sex are powerful, that people who don't have enough sex are boring, and that sex is a useful tool for getting what you want in life. That's a lot of messaging! But the way it impacts you (or not) is likely to be shaped by that second circle: the communities you're involved in. If your family attends an ultraconservative church, you're likely to grow up internalizing a lot of society's more damning ideas of sex (and all the shame that goes with them). If you grow up in a more open community, that negative messaging might roll right off your back. Finally, you have that innermost circle: the attitudes you develop based on your own experiences. If you're caught with porn under your mattress and punished for it, you may develop one perspective (whether it's shame or the more "rebellious" bent toward erotic humiliation). But if the person who finds the porn uses it as an opportunity to talk openly with you about safe and consensual sex, that may lead to a whole different attitude.

In short, while everyone starts with the same basic messaging—the outer circle, or the base of the iceberg, you could survey a hundred different people and get a hundred different responses about the sources of their kinks. All of these are based on the messaging they heard from their more direct communities and, most importantly, their own personal experiences with those negative cultural contexts we're all exposed to.

FLIPPING THE SCRIPT

In short, erotic humiliation could be considered a way of "cosplaying" oppression. Sometimes it's about exploring scenarios you've never experienced, but often it's about exaggerating or emphasizing some kind of oppression you *have* experienced in your life in order to take back control, using your own (real or perceived) shortcomings or insecurities as a source of power.

Take "small penis humiliation," for example: if the world has told you all your life that having a small penis makes you "less than," one way to rebel against it is to embrace that shame as something that turns you on instead. You're flipping the cultural script.

Another example—and one of my favorites—of how erotic humiliation flips the cultural script is the word "slut." The reason the word "slut" is so powerful (even when it's used lovingly in kink) is because of all the cultural context that goes with it. The use of the word in the "real world" is almost always intended to be derogatory and to elicit feelings of shame and humiliation. That's exactly what allows kinksters to flip it on its head and make it sexy. Let me illustrate:

When I was a teenager and was kissing boys, the other girls were very upset with that and were calling me a slut—and not with a sense of admiration or empowerment. They used it to mean that I was a bad person or someone of lesser value. When I kissed a boy and got called a slut, it was not to celebrate me in any way. Now, when I call my submissives sluts, there is certainly a reference to the derogatory nature in the outside world and my own experience with it. But with my submissives, I reframe and reclaim "slut" to mean something new in the context of erotic humiliation, which is ultimately an empowering celebration. "Yeah, you're a slut. You like it. I like it. Let's see what this slut can do." Yay!

Contrast those teenaged girls' attitudes with the cultural understanding of the word "slut" at an event I have taught at many times, Dark Odyssey Fusion, where more than a thousand perverts take over a campground. People fuck on the grass and tie each other to trees and pee on each other out-side of the mess hall. It's a paradise for kinky, dirty people.

Every year they used to give an award for "camp slut." People voted, and it was very serious. People campaigned all weekend long. "Do you need a blowjob? Can I offer a bit of a muff dive? Anyone want to have an orgy? I'm going for camp slut. Who needs some sexy kinky action?" All genders and sexual orientations were welcome—we had sluts across the spectrum! A few years ago, they were giving out the camp awards at the mess hall, which is big enough to fit the entire camp. The woman who had won "Camp Slut"—and she earned it, let me tell you—was at the back of this huge hall when they called her name.

As she walked up to the front stage to accept her rib-bon, people began to chant, "Slut! Slut! Slut! Slut! Slut!" First it was just a small group of people, and then it was naturally taken up by the entire hall. There was love and adoration and respect in that word. Empowerment. Within the context of, "But you're so dirty!" or, "You're doing dirty, filthy, 'bad' things," there was a much more powerful layer of, "Yay! We love it! We love you!" "Yay for sluts!"

Words are powerful. But in the context of erotic humilia-tion, we can redirect their power and use it for our benefit. And this is true for any "controversial" or negative or unsavory cultural context you can think of. By using the larger world context and adding an underlying or overlying emphasis on acceptance and affection, amusement, and love, we can turn those negative feelings of shame into erotically charged humiliation.

CREATING THE BUBBLE
BALANCING CULTURAL CONTEXT WITH EROTIC EMPOWERMENT

The cultural context of the "outside world" really is important—it's what makes this kink possible at all—but it is the layer of affection, care, and follow-through between partners that enables us to balance that cultural context with erotic empowerment and engage in happy, healthy humiliation (as opposed to harmful shaming). I think of it as being in **the bubble**.

You may have heard of relationship expert Stan Tatkin's concept of "The Couple Bubble." The gist is that, in a healthy relationship, partners can create a "bubble" in which they can continue to grow, both independently and as a unit, while feeling safe and protected from complicating factors outside of that bubble. (You can read more about it online or in his 2011 book, *Wired for Love*.)

Being "in the bubble" with kink is a similar concept. What we're trying to do is create a bubble that we go into at will. It's a bit like Glinda the Good Witch's bubble, where we can see the outside world but we're protected from its pressures and judgments. Being in this bubble allows us to take the context of the outside world and change it to suit our purposes. We only bring in with us what we need—primarily trust, respect, and affection for our partner—and we leave the rest outside. Just like Glinda, we can use the bubble to go anywhere.

I do not enjoy anything that causes me to lose respect for myself, causes me to lose the respect of my partner, causes me to lose respect for my partner, or damages the self esteem of either my partner or myself. However, done right it can be freeing to lose one's self deeper in play, giving permission to say or do things that would normally be reluctantly done (if at all).

- Matt G

KERNEL KINK

When someone comes to you and says they're into humiliation, you'll see how little information that statement is actually giving you. You need more information about who they are, what they're into, and what level they want to play at. That introduction is where your discussion begins, not where it ends.

After all, we have to remember that what one person finds erotically humiliating, another person might find liberating (or genuinely horrifying). In order to humiliate an individual, the key is really understanding their personal context. There's a story you need to hear that they have been telling inside their head. Tease that story out and you'll know everything you need. That's what is going to dictate whether or not they find an action to be embarrassing, humiliating, or degrading. Great humiliation does not come from the orders you give in a contrived scenario or from some external force. One of the biggest misconceptions about humiliation play is that it starts from the action—the idea that establishing a typically "humiliating" scenario will achieve the results both players want, when in reality, it may lead to a totally different response. Rather, great humiliation comes from the sub's *responses* to the scenario. It comes from within.

That's why, nearly twenty years ago I developed the concept of a **kernel kink**, which describes the core emotional aspect of your kink, the *why* rather than the *how*, and the desired *feeling* rather than an *action*.

Why? Because a single action could produce a myriad of feelings. Consider crawling, for example. It's one action, but there are different ways to do it that make it feel completely different. You could take up as little space as possible, hunching your shoulders and trying to fold in on yourself, or you could crawl as if you're a lion stalking her prey. Same action, two totally different feelings. What one person finds to be low-level embarrassment might be hardcore degradation for someone else. That's why we have to get down to the kernel kink—what way, exactly, do you want to feel?—before we can identify the activities that will make for satisfying erotic humiliation experiences.

The reason for this is that what someone finds humiliating is most often associated with the biggest taboos in their own life, whether those taboos come from cultural, familial, or personal values. The humiliation comes from experiencing pleasure from these "bad" things—from these experiences that are socially supposed to be negative. Gender dynamics and body functions are two common examples, but because everybody's values and taboos are different, there is no singular set of rules about which activities are humiliating or not. It is entirely determined by the players involved.

I frequently incorporate some element of humiliation in my play style. Whether it is in the context of a loving relationship, a play partner or just a single scene, I find it important to engage the mind and humiliation works directly in the subject's brain.

- Mr Ogre

Here's another clear example: satin panties on straight men.

For most straight, cis-men, being "forced" to wear panties is completely emasculating. Those men have typically been told their whole lives that such frilly and silky fabrics are only for sissies, and that they should avoid being sissies at all costs. This creates an incredibly strong taboo that can often be used in a consensual, erotically humiliating scene.

However, that sort of aversion to their own attraction is not the only response possible. I have a male submissive who presents as genderqueer in kink spaces but usually presents as **cis-het** guy in public. When I put panties on him, he prances around singing, "I'm in panties, sexy panties!" He may find the experience pleasurable, but he is so not humiliated! He tells me enthusiastically, "I love being in my panties." But when I put those same panties on another, actually cis-het guy, he's likely to think, "Oh my God, my manhood has been stolen from me." How the person feels about the action is what makes it sexy and powerful.

Why is this? It's because humiliation is 100 percent psychological. While in something like impact play, the physicality of an act alone may be the erotic trigger, in humiliation play, it's *the psychological response to the action* that makes it sexual, and that's an incredibly personal thing.

For instance, "sploshing" is messy play where you throw food at people or dump buckets of, say, cake batter on their head. For somebody who finds that humiliating, the power lies in the mental experience, as opposed to just the fact that there's goop on their body. In fact, there are plenty of people into sploshing who do *not* find it humiliating. They have a different emotional state associated with it, such as feeling joyful or silly.

To me, to be erotically humiliating, it has to be somewhat realistic and has to be a mind game on some level, a game of wits. Yelling rote insults is sort of flat and meaningless to me. So, even though I marked a lot of these [activities] on the first [negotiation] list as very humiliating, many of them are not erotically humiliating to me [as a dominant]. I like to keep a calm demeanor, never raising my voice, slowly twisting the guy's mind, using his desires against him.

- Lanie

You can't humiliate somebody with something that they don't find humiliating. If you're trying to humiliate someone who doesn't find satin panties humiliating, you're going to be frustrated, and they're going to be thinking, "Seriously? Is this it?" and you might just end up watching television instead of playing, which makes my pervert heart sad. But once you find something that works, there is a lot of room to play, even within just one activity.

COMMON REASONS TO EXPLORE EROTIC HUMILIATION

I've realized that lots of humiliating things turn me on, and that's okay, especially because there are other people who like putting me into (and then safely removing me from) those humiliating situations.

- E

When I get interviewed by the media, they inevitably ask, "What type of person is attracted to BDSM?" My response is that it isn't one social class or one ethnic group. Identity is made up of puzzle pieces, and sexuality is a hard one to fit. What people desire—certainly in the BDSM world—runs up against preconceived notions of what society says is okay. More importantly, though, it runs up against preconceived notions of what they think they should want, or what they believe they are allowed to have. The result is that the BDSM community is made up of people who think hard about these puzzle pieces in themselves and usually have to break some "rules" and come up with their own solutions to find sexual satisfaction. So my consistent response is that the "typical" person in the BDSM world tends to be cerebral and more imaginative than the average person. The "typical" kinkster is somebody who is creative. This is something I know anecdotally, from experience, but it's also been studied formally, with a 2013 study by Andreas Wismeijer and Marcel van Assen, published in the *Journal of Sexual Medicine*, finding that, compared with non-BDSM participants, BDSM enthusiasts are less neurotic, more extraverted, and more open to new experiences. The same study found BDSM participants to have a better overall subjective well-being and to be stronger both psychologically and interpersonally. Far from that maladjusted stereotype.

So, why harness that creativity and intelligence into erotic humiliation? There are lots of reasons, and they're different for everybody. But let's look at a few I hear commonly, and then we'll explore the different reasons someone might be interested in erotic psychological torment, whether as a dominant or as a submissive.

While I'm a firm believer that kinky orientation can be innate, as I mentioned, it's also fairly common for kinksters to have a catalyst experience from which they develop a fetish for, or erotic interest in, humiliation. There are some people who can trace that interest back to a particular memory. Some people have an experience in their youth that inspires a lifetime of perversion. A moment's humiliation in front of the class, perhaps, or an instance of unintentional exposure. These experiences often happen early in life and are associated with intense emotions and a person's earliest sexual feelings.

Many find themselves attempting to recreate the experience without the risk or involvement of others later in life, to recapture that bright mental impression of humiliation, attention, and vulnerability. This may lead to developing a relationship with a partner or a professional who can help the individual rebuild that experience under safe and consensual circumstances. In this way, erotic experiences and memories can be relived indefinitely, and their strange glory never fades. A common refrain is that kink can be therapeutic, but it's not therapy.

> *There was a time I felt a lot of shame over my kinks and how they related to my trauma. But as I've overcome trauma, my kinks almost feel earned. I am a strong woman, and my kinks do not control me. They belong to me.*
>
> *- Anonymous*

For some, it's the facing of fear that is powerful and attractive. The fear of acting "improperly," the fear of confronting social taboo, the fear of their desires not being "acceptable," the fear of being vulnerable and "stripped of defenses," the fear of being removed from their comfort zone...all of these are fears that create a powerful psychological dynamic.

> As long as it's consenting, why not enjoy? Plus, I believe that a lot of subs enjoy humiliation as a way of owning their shame—enjoying the taboo and the words and things that hurt them when they know it's for pleasure. Like a rollercoaster is about owning fear and scary bodily feelings.
>
> - English Leather Master

Often, again, it's simply the rush of embracing taboo. It's a feeling of, "Oh! We're not supposed to do it. Let's do it now with costumes and special props!"

> I like the psychological reading of people. Finding those mental pleasure-pain buttons and trying to find the perfect time to press them.
>
> - EQ

FOR SUBMISSIVES: WHY WOULD ANYONE LET SOMEONE DO THIS STUFF TO THEM?

There can be a wide range of reactions to erotic humiliation play. Blushing, feeling nauseous, feeling dizzy, wanting to run and hide, avoiding eye contact, being at a loss for words, and, of course, feeling turned on. In fact, one reason submissives enjoy humiliation is that the physiological response to being the recipient of erotic embarrassment is almost identical to traditional arousal. Your heart beats faster. You get flushed.

You get really nervous. You can't focus. Your palms get sweaty. There's an actual physical experience that supports the mental/psychological/emotional experience happening.

> *I "sub out" when humiliation has eroded my sense of having any control and I am left feeling helpless, embarrassed, small, and completely in awe of my Sir. It's an expression of power that she has over me. I can't fight back, I can't resist and I just have to become smaller and smaller as it continues. It's a little scary, but wonderful.*
>
> *- P*

These are some of the answers that have come up from submissives in my workshops when they're asked what they get out of it:

- "Because it turns me on."
- "To prove I can take it."
- "Puts me in my place."
- "I love the loss of control."
- "It's a permission slip to do taboo things. I'm not *doing* it. I'm being 'forced' to do it."
- "Suffering is an act of service."
- "It makes me feel vulnerable."
- "I feel a cathartic release."
- "It can be done anywhere, and it doesn't need any other tools."
- "Being seen—that I'm really acknowledged and the focus is on me."

It can be surprisingly cathartic to experience a consensual annihilation of self. When you put not only your bodily safety but also your mental well-being in the hands of somebody else, there is definitely an extra layer of risk, but there's also an extra rush. This is another reason I think humiliation play is really scary (and thus also enticing) for a lot of people.

> I used to feel shame around my desires, like I was a fucked-up person for wanting someone to degrade me, or like it went against my feminist beliefs and that I was a traitor to my sex and women's rights. But as I've gotten older, the shame has faded away and the self judgment is gone. I couldn't give two shits about what anyone else thinks or how society defines feminism. I can be both a depraved slut who likes to be a human toilet and a feminist, all in one beautiful package.
>
> - Rose

Some submissives find that running headlong into their insecurities and anxieties in erotic play allowed them to release the power those emotions were holding over the rest of their lives. It acts as a sort of (very unofficial) exposure therapy.

> It can actually help me feel more confident to play with my insecurities, because talking about it takes away some of the power of it.
>
> - Ella Notte

> i personally feel that when I'm down and have low confidence, a session of humiliation, while

*[momentarily] making me feel worse while it's hap-
pening, kind of jump-starts my endorphins and i
feel more confident after being strong and enduring the humiliation.*

- M

*It kinda takes me back to [my youth]. I was left out
of a party and felt humiliated. Revisiting humiliation is therapeutic. I can face the feelings and that
makes me stronger and it makes the negative
memories lose their power.*

- Angelia

FOR DOMINANTS: WHY WOULD ANYONE DO THESE THINGS TO SOMEONE ELSE?

That combination of risk and rush is a powerful enticement
for dominants as well. After all, it's a major responsibility to
ensure that I don't do nerve damage while I'm tying you up;
it's just as big a responsibility to ensure that I don't send you
to therapy afterward.

But at an even more basic level, the fact is that it's super
fun and super taboo, and it's really exciting to play at being
mean in a way that is actually ethical and appreciated. The
power of forcing somebody (within a consensual arrangement) to do taboo things is gratifying and liberating; it allows
dominants to express parts of themselves that are not often
acceptable in life. For me, it's fun to be mean simply because
I'm not supposed to be. I love the taboo of it. Like many
women, I was raised to be a "very nice girl." I have struggled
against the definition of that my whole life. I do believe that

I am a nice person (and people who know me would agree), but having an approved, consensual, and ethical outlet to be a total cunt is important for my personal psychological well-being! That's my reason, but there can be a lot of other reasons, too.

> *I'm a really nice girl in general, but it's his wonderful and lovely natural desire to be ridiculed that brings it out of me.*
>
> *- Miss JW*

For example, along with loving to make people follow my commands. I also have an absurdity kink. Life is funny. It's really fucking funny, and what we kinksters do is even funnier, so I embrace that. I love to use humiliation and use power dynamics to embrace those things.

At the beginning of my prodomme career, my apartment flooded, filling with literally six feet of water in thirty seconds and destroying everything I owned. I had three sessions booked for the next day. I called two of them and canceled, then called the only one who was into humiliation. "You're going to come to the hotel," I told him. "I've had a really shitty couple of days, and I need to release some pent-up emotion, and you're my submissive, so I want you to take it. What do you think?"

He gave his consent, so when he arrived at the hotel, I went to the kitchen and asked for a dozen raw eggs. I took them out to the parking lot and I threw eggs at him until I was giggling like a maniac and feeling much better about things because...life is fucked. What are you going to do?

For him, that was about a submissive, devotional service that he could provide for me. I needed to have a release—the activity was literally nothing to do with any specific activities he had asked for or what he came in to request or experience. But I said, "I need to do this thing. You say you're submissive to me. This is how you can best serve me," and he consented. I used our power dynamic as the main focus, although I'd chosen him because he was into humiliation, so I knew he'd still like it—and so did I! By the time I was done, I was laughing out loud!

In case you're inspired, here are two quick tips for egg-throwing!

- If you're going to throw eggs at somebody, break them first because they don't actually break on human beings and it's really frustrating when you're throwing them and it just falls with a thud where they break on the ground!

- If you're going to crack eggs over the top of someone's head, make sure that you don't get goop in the eyes or any cuts. This particular submissive was bald-headed, so it dripped down the side of his skull, adding another layer of fun for me.

I really, really, really love the idea of taking a strong man into my hands and molding him like putty, bringing him down a peg or five.

- Lanie

Hilarity aside, I also derive a sense of pride from dominance. I feel super proud of my submissives when they get through really humiliating experiences. They know that, and they want me to feel that pride, so they push through even when something is difficult for them. That's a really satisfying and impressive feeling. (And pride aside, I'm rather flattered that people will sacrifice their dignity for me.)

The moment when you fulfill a fantasy for yourself or your partner is a really special one, and knowing that I've had these great moments or made those moments for others is very meaningful to me.

- Foot Rest Boy

Here are more reasons that have come up from dominants in my workshops:

- "It's a way of understanding someone. If you know what humiliates them, it's like a way of breaking down a person and really knowing them."
- "It's really intimate."
- "I like creating the conflict between shame and excitement."
- "It's intellectually stimulating."
- "I like to help someone access a part of themselves that they might not be comfortable with."
- "I love the cathartic release on the top side."
- "I'm an emotional sadist."
- "The ability to flex my creative muscles is most certainly there in humiliation."
- "It doesn't leave any obvious physical marks."
- "You can show someone however low they go, you'll always love them anyway."

- "To show how in control you are."

As we've discussed, a dominant who is engaging in healthy play has the utmost affection for their submissive. But even at that, some dominants do occasionally take a step back and say, "Oh my god, what am I doing?" This is completely natural. We've spent many years being told by society that this sort of behavior isn't acceptable. So, as a dominant, if you're struggling with conflicted feelings about humiliating your partner, find an affirmation that can help you remember that this is what they've asked for. This is what they want. This is something that you've negotiated together.

> I would've loved to answer "I'm 98% fine with it. It's so very natural for both of us, but still there's a little voice inside my head that sometimes wonders what's wrong with me? Let's face it: I enjoy hurting the one I love more than anyone or anything on this planet. When you put it out simple like that it doesn't make much sense! Of course our play is always done with mutual consent and I would never hurt or humiliate him in damaging or disrespectful ways—you know those that break your soul instead of being sexually gratifying. But then I think it's good that there's that little bit of sense and doubt left in me, keeping me in check and making me go through and rethink my actions over him.
>
> - Miss JW

There is so much in our world that we don't control. To have specific experiences with negotiated boundaries where we can consciously give up or take control, to make that choice, is an incredibly powerful act. This all just proves my point earlier about how many different paths we take to get to this experience of humiliation. The bottom line is, for whatever reason, it makes clits wet, cocks hard, and genitals happy. That's just it. Human beings are complicated creatures!

> *I enjoy seeing how much my submissive gets turned on by being humiliated. Teasing and degrading him builds a sexual tension that I find titillating. It gives me a rush.*
>
> *- Princess Annika*

Particularly as a dominant, when you turn the corner of understanding that what you're doing is giving your partner something they want, it becomes crueler to deny them than to actually do it to them. This is a concept that was pivotal for me in letting my **humiliatrix** self out: the realization that denying someone what they've asked me to do to them (as long as it's within my own comfort zone)—no matter how taboo and humiliating it may be—is actually more cruel, whereas giving it to them is a gesture of affection and connection.

> *Being with her when she feels like doing it is incredible. It's as much about seeing her be powerful as it is about losing control. When a woman can comfortably humiliate a man it shows confidence and strength. When she can do it in a way that achieves the balance they both need, then that shows control and intelligence. I also love it when she gets creative and the improvisation is*

surprising... All I can think about is 'what's coming next?'. The anticipation builds with hit after hit.

- P

WHEN DOES AROUSAL HAPPEN?

As you read about me giggling madly while throwing raw eggs at my submissive in the parking lot, you may have wondered, "Where's the eroticism in that?" Good question.

The eroticism of humiliating encounters—whether they're as absurd as my egg-throwing or far more serious—really boils down to the power structure that's being put on clear display. After all, the human species, and all the cultural contexts we've grown up with, are rooted deeply in power. So when a sub truly realizes what they've allowed (or even requested) someone to do or say to them, it often makes them feel powerless in a way that's, counterintuitively, highly empowering. It creates a sense of incredulity at the power on display. For some subs, what's most attractive is their own powerlessness, while others are more in awe of the other person's power. (No, it's not linear, and no, it's not a clear-cut cause and effect. That's the biggest obstacle to this whole thing: you're either attracted to playing with power through humiliation or you're not, and if you're not, it's hard to understand, even academically.)

All that said, a lot of feelings can come up during the humiliation experience itself, and eroticism isn't always one of them. For subs, these may include smallness, vulnerability, exposure, dirtiness, etc. For dominants, they may include power, amusement, and emotional sadism. The intensity can be distracting from feeling turned on in the moment. In fact, many people who are interested in humiliation on the submissive side find that the eroticizism comes *before* the scene, in the anticipation, as well as afterward, when they're looking back on an experience, rather than when they're actually having the experience. When "in it," the focus can be on getting through the overwhelming feelings being brought up. Then after the fact it's like, "*Whoa*, it's so sexy that I was so overwhelmed/helpless/etc."

> *Before it's like the anticipation you would get going up a roller coaster, or getting strapped in to bungee jump. Then during it it's the biggest rush like when you get to the top of the coaster and just are starting to go over the edge.*
>
> *- Lincoln B.*

Then again, many people are turned on before, during, *and* after a humiliation session! I think this is one of the most complicated aspects of humiliation play: not only where and how, but *when* eroticization takes place. Of course, there's no one right answer as long as the core aspects of healthy kink are being observed (more about that in the next chapter). Often, submissives "hate to love" humiliation experiences— not in a negative way, but in the sense of a love/hate relationship where there's a strong attraction that inexplicably grows over time.

> *I love the dark places, and the darker we go, the more turned on I get.*
>
> *- Belle*

ONLY SEEK OUT THE WHY IF YOU WANT TO

Some people like to spend time figuring out their sexuality, like putting together a puzzle of themselves. For these people, the unanswered question of why they enjoy humiliating or being humiliated can be a real obstacle to getting to the pleasure of the experience. Many others simply come to accept themselves, find a healthy outlet, and never go back to unpack the "why" ever again. Still others are adamantly against exploring where their kinks come from because they fear that understanding them will ruin the attraction. (I find this concern to be especially common among submissives, anecdotally.) It's certainly possible to become desensitized to something through the kind of repeated exposure that comes with understanding it, but more often than not, I find the opposite to be true. When we understand our kinks, we're actually able to explore them more deeply, more powerfully, and more erotically.

> As i get more comfortable in myself i find my
> erotic humiliation interests broadening. The more
> i love myself, the more i can allow someone else to
> degrade me within a scene.
>
> - Erin Quinn

All that said, it's entirely up to you to decide what path you'll choose. The question of why you are into humiliation—why anyone is—is one that you may or may not feel compelled to answer. If you're having consensual experiences with a consenting adult partner and you come out of them feeling positive, then it really may not matter whether or not you ever made a connection or identified the reason. Spend time on it if you want, or just get back to having kinky fun!

If you're waiting for someone to give you permission to try these things and feel good about them, I hereby grant it with all the authority of my position as a professional connoisseur of kink. I am here to tell you that the subtlest whip is wielded by the psyche. No judgment: find what works for you, negotiate consent, and go for it! I have done this professionally for a very long time, and I have seen everything from people who had triggering experiences in their youth to people who simply don't know and don't care why this gets them off. That's all fine. The bottom line is, if you're doing it with a consenting adult and you're having fun, then what's stopping you? Go for it.

> *I think the desire was probably always there but accepting it and allowing it to happen took a little time. The deep trust I have in my partner allowed me to feel the humiliation, but feel safe as well. As a submissive I was in situations that were potentially embarrassing, and she took the opportunity to tease me a little during, or after the scene. For some time it was just very playful, but then I started asking her to go further with the names she used for me, and what she wanted me to do. Be careful what you ask for perhaps, but I loved it when she first went hard at me and every time since.*
>
> *- P*

CHAPTER 3

THE ETHICS OF PSYCHOLOGICAL TORMENT PLAY

I think it is important to stay mindful, observant, and even doubtful because of the potential risks to other's or one's own morality. As edge play, it's a bit like being a gymnast who needs to be aware of her fitness and body condition while practicing challenging moves.

- CRAVINGS

HAVE YOU EVER WONDERED IF it's ethical to do humiliation play? It can be a confusing question from both outside and inside the play. How can anyone tell the difference between sexy adventures and abusive behavior when it all looks the same on the surface?

We'll explore all of this in this chapter, but as you read, please remember two things: First, I'm not a trained psychologist or a trained philosopher! I can't tell you what is "right" or "wrong" for you or anyone else (beyond the foundation of consent). Second, everything in this book—and in the entire realm of ethical kink—is about play that occurs between two consenting *adults*. Playing with minors is *never* ethical. Period. End of story. And even when we're playing with adults, consent can be more complicated to gauge than a simple yes or no. We'll cover what all consent entails in the next chapter, but in brief: all parties must be in the right headspace to communicate clearly and confidently about what they do and do not what to do. If it's a maybe, it's a no.

FIVE KEY INDICATORS OF ETHICAL PLAY

There is a *huge* difference between someone exploring the edges of a partner's psyche in a consensual erotic humiliation scene and someone truly just being mean. Remember the bubble we talked about in the last chapter? Well, when someone uses their partner's soft spots and vulnerabilities against them *outside* of that bubble, play becomes abuse. And when it's abusive, humiliation play goes much, much further than simply being mean. But how can you tell where that line is, or whether it's been crossed? First, remember to always listen to your gut. If you're in a situation you suspect may be abusive, take it seriously. If you're not sure, consider these five key differentiators between ethical humiliation play (green flags) and abuse (red flags).

CONSENT

Consent is the absolutely number one key component to making sure that what we're doing is healthy, happy humiliation. Consent is by far *the* most important aspect of ethical erotic humiliation.

Some submissives (and dominants, too) worry that because a sub has asked or agreed to be humiliated, somehow it isn't "true" humiliation. That's not only bullshit, but it's also dangerous. The consent and desire to engage is an absolutely necessary part of healthy humiliation, and **non-consent** is an immediate dealbreaker. However, for many, the aspect of **consensual non-consent** is important to the experience of humiliation, so you'll see the word "forced" fairly frequently in this book. Even when you're playing with the idea of force, there still needs to be a solid foundation of consent, negotiation, and communication for it to be erotic, and not abusive.

GREEN FLAGS

- You and your partner are both in a headspace that allows you to think clearly and rationally about what you do and do not want to do.

- Both of you have enthusiastically agreed to engage in play.

- You've both communicated your own limits and boundaries and have agreed to respect each other's.

- If you're the dominant, you understand that you're not dragging your submissive through the mud but waltzing with them (even though you've agreed that you get to belittle them for being an inept dancer and humiliate them for stepping on your feet).

RED FLAGS

- Either you or your partner is under the influence, exhausted, too inexperienced to understand what you're agreeing to, or otherwise in the wrong head-space to be able to give clear and well-thought-out consent. (More on barriers to consent in the next chapter.)

- If you're the submissive, you're hesitant to express your desires and boundaries for fear of "topping from the bottom."

- If you're the dominant, you hold the (false and dangerous) belief that the only way to truly humiliate the sub is to blow past their boundaries and use language or actions they've indicated as hard limits.

CONTEXT

Context makes a huge difference in play versus abuse. Without the context of "kinkiness," we're just a bunch of people hitting each other with expensive sticks and mops. For example, I know plenty of people who are very into kinky, erotic humiliation who do not like being dressed down by their boss in their office in front of people. The idea that just any humiliating experience is automatically going to provide you with jerk-off material is not true. The context of kink play includes the environment, the relationship between players, timing, consent, etc.

But even within the context of kinkiness, pre-negotiated erotic play can go horribly wrong if it happens in the wrong place or at the wrong time. For example, I own my submissive, wimpy, so fully that I can humiliate him in intense, intense ways in so many environments. And yet, I would never go into his work and say, "Hey, Piggy, get over here and smell my fart." That's one of my favorite activities, and it's one he consents to in many other situations, but in that particular context, it's no longer play—it's abuse.

GREEN FLAGS

- After you've both given consent, you've made sure that the environment is appropriate and the situation is one you both desire.

- You both understand where and when it is and is not appropriate to engage in play.

RED FLAGS

- If you're a submissive, you're being dressed down by somebody or you're being humiliated in a way that is not erotic to you. The issue may be consent, but it could also be that the context is wrong.

- If you're a dominant, you're shaming or breaking someone outside of the negotiated kinky context.

INTENTION

Intention comes back to the cruelty stereotype we talked about. Yes, cruel things can happen in erotic humiliation, but what makes it play instead of abuse is that the submissive knows the dominant is tearing them down in order to build them up and that, ultimately, the experience will be pleasurable for both parties. If you're questioning whether your intentions are ethical, just start by asking yourself this very pop-ular question among kinksters: *"Why does the idea of doing something that might ruin my life turn me on so much?"*

For dominants, ethical intentions are about ultimate satis-faction—not just a desire to be cruel. For example, I like to turn my subs small so that they can feel big in that smallness. There's a difference between telling someone, "You are tiny and useless," and leaving it at that versus telling them, "You are tiny and use-less, and I love you like that." Because no matter how this stuff looks superficially, we want people to come out on the other side happy it happened. We'll talk about aftercare in depth later on, but remember that no dominant or partner could provide the kind of necessary support and affection to bring a submis-sive safely out of a humiliating encounter if they were motivated by feelings of malice or abuse. This balance is vital to the differ-ence between real humiliation and humiliation play.

> *With an educated partner that understands that they may break [me] down, but must rebuild [me] even stronger than when they found [me]. I adore when Hubs calls me His dirty slut or whore and uses me. But afterwards he will take me in His arms and whisper loving endearments and tell me how proud He was of me.*
>
> *- TaRt*

It's easy to talk about how the dominant's intentions can impact the ethics (or lack thereof) of a scene, but the submis-sive's can, as well. If you're approaching erotic humiliation as an opportunity for arousal and sexual satisfaction, great! But if you're coming in with depression or low self-esteem and a desire for self-harm or punishment, then it's no longer ethical play, and not only are you harming yourself, but you're also putting your partner in danger and breaking their trust.

GREEN FLAGS

- As the dominant, you want to break your sub down and then build them up in some way, or at least pull them through.

- As the sub, you leave the experience feeling satisfied, respected, and cared for—no matter how gnarly things got in the scene.

RED FLAGS

- If you're a dominant whose intention is to leave your sub broken and then be done with them, then you're an abusive asshole.

- If you're a sub and you leave the situation feeling shitty (in general or about something specific), you may simply need to rethink your aftercare plan (see chapter 4), but it may also be that your dom's intentions weren't healthy to begin with.

- If you're submissive and your intention comes from a negative place such as a desire for self-harm, then you're turning play into abuse.

TRUST

It's clear that the submissive has to have absolute trust in the dominant, but this trust must go both ways. While submissives need to feel confident their dominants aren't going to put them in actual physical or emotional danger, dominants need to trust that their subs have done everything in their power to avoid leaving any invisible minefields on the playground. As the dominant, I need to trust my submissive, because I'm going to do some (consensually kinky) fucked up shit to them, and I don't want any surprises. I'm not going to feel comfortable laying into someone, even in the way that they've asked, if I can't trust that they'll communicate with me or that they've been honest about their level of experience.

> *I experienced a trigger with a previous partner. I was ordered to exercise in front of him while he judged and heckled me. Having body issues, I became overwhelmed with shame and I collapsed on the floor into tears and "red-ed out." We discussed what happened, but in the end I asked that we not play in that way in the future. We were not long-term play partners and I had not developed the trust in him that I needed to engage in such an emotionally heavy form of humiliation for me.*
>
> *- Ashley Rose*
>
> *I'm in a D/s relationship and, once trust was firmly established, I began to crave humiliation. Humiliation cements our love. I trust Him enough to let Him strip away all my control and dignity, and I know, because it's reinforced each time we play, that He loves me despite seeing me in that "state." As someone who generally thinks the world will implode if anyone sees my vulnerability, letting him see my dignity fall apart and knowing He still loves me is nurturing and healing.*
>
> *- Anonymous*

Without trust, ethical humiliation is not possible. If you don't fully trust your play partner—or you suspect they don't trust you—then you should take a look at what's missing and at what your motivations are for doing what you're doing.

GREEN FLAGS

- You're confident your partner has fully communicated their boundaries and desires.

- Your partner has a track record of respecting limits, sticking to negotiated activities, and communicating when something isn't going well.

RED FLAGS

- Your partner has been hesitant to share desires, limits, and experiences.

- Your partner has a track record of "slipping up" when it comes to boundaries.

- Your gut says something isn't quite right.

COMMUNICATION

Appropriate communication is the final aspect of ethical kinky experiences. We talk about communication extensively in the next two chapters, but for starters, these green and red flags can help you distinguish between healthy communication and indicators of abuse.

GREEN FLAGS

- You both know your voices, opinions, desires, and limits are respected and necessary to mutually satisfying play.

- You're both committed to communicating honestly and consistently, even when expressing your needs might delay or "ruin" a scene.

RED FLAGS

- You're afraid to express yourself to your partner.

- You're not interested in hearing what your partner has to say.

- You'd rather push forward in a scene than "ruin" it by checking in with your partner or asking for a change, even when something isn't right.

SO, IS IT ABUSE?

In short, when someone is abusive, the intention is to tear the other person down, to shame them into feeling genuinely, deeply bad about themselves. The feelings that come to mind are oppressive, negative, hateful, malicious, and hurtful.

Abuse comes from the abuser's need to feel bigger or stronger than they are. Putting others down or controlling them is the only way abusers feel better about themselves. Abuse stems from the abusers' insecurities, and there are big red flags that you can look for, even if the above indicators aren't giving you a clear picture:

1. There has been no negotiation, no expression of desire, and no consent.

2. The whole experience feels emotionally violent and leaves you feeling negative about yourself.

3. You negotiated this type of play within a consensual scene but your boundaries aren't being respected.

4. The other person is disrespectful, rude, hurtful, or outright vicious on a regular basis with no concern about how it makes you feel and no regard for pre-negotiated contexts or settings.

5. The memories of the experience continue to make you feel sad or upset.

A person doesn't have to be physically hit to be abused. When one partner nonconsensually verbally assaults the other, that *is* abuse. Even if it happens only once, even if it's unintentional, it is still an abusive experience, and we'll talk about how (and whether) to move forward in chapter 4. If it happens more than once, then it is ongoing emotional cruelty and *not* erotic humiliation.

He said something that triggered an extremely negative response—which for me is usually freezing up. I simply asked him not to say that again and why it didn't work for me, and he apologized and cuddled me and has never said it again.

- Victoria Harrington

WHY YOU CAN'T JUST TRY ANYTHING AND SEE IF IT WORKS

To some kinksters—often the inexperienced or the less responsible players—all the preparation and communication that precedes a healthy scene feels like too much "work" or a waste of time. These folks often ask me why we can't just "start trying things" to "see what works."

The short answer is that that's abuse. The longer answer is that this approach is inherently unethical because, if you're just doing a bunch of abusive things to somebody without any idea of how it's going to impact them, then you're missing a lot of those key indicators of ethical kink: there's no communication, not nearly enough consent, no opportunity to build trust, and no indication that your intention is ethical. Whether you're a dominant proposing this scattershot approach or a submissive asking for it, you're setting up both players for a highly unhealthy experience in which any number of triggers—from the mild to the crippling—are likely to be tripped. That's why negotiation is so paramount that I've dedicated an entire chapter to it (chapter 5).

> *Early on in our relationship (eight years), my partner slapped me in the face and I got PISSED. I thought about breaking up with him! But we talked about it and decided it was a hard limit and we never did it again. So we resolved it with communication.*
>
> *- Kendra*

BDSM CAN BE THERAPEUTIC, BUT IT'S NOT THERAPY

As we've discussed, it can be cathartic and even therapeutic to reframe past negative experiences through erotic humiliation. However, erotic humiliation—or any sexual play, for that matter—is not meant to be a substitute for actual therapy. If you're revisiting truly traumatic situations, it's important that you don't just take that on yourself or put it on your partner's shoulders. Unless one of you is an actual, trained psychologist, that's both incredibly unethical and incredibly dangerous. Using kink to work through trauma is possible, but it requires careful research and expert help. Kinky play can be a way to work through trauma, for both dominants and submissives, but only with the guidance of a kink-friendly therapist. (If you need direction, the National Coalition for Sexual Freedom has a list of kink-aware professionals at kapprofessionals.org.)

When and if you do decide to play with unresolved and potentially triggering experiences (with the help and support of an expert), it's important to keep my pool metaphor in mind and hang out in the shallow end as long as necessary—and maybe even longer. When you do increase intensity, it must be done carefully and with knowledge and respect of limits. It's great to use erotic humiliation as a cathartic release, but make sure that you're not just running rampant into behavior that may create new trauma or reopen old wounds.

Humiliation can be a great tool, but make sure that you're using it intelligently. It is not enough to wave the wand and say the magic words. You cannot subject someone to one kinky interaction and expect it to heal old trauma. I wish it worked that way, because I would be a millionaire. "I spit in your face! You're cured!" I'm damn good, but I'm not that good. Neither are you.

CHAPTER 4

HOW TO HAVE HAPPY, HEALTHY HUMILIATION

*[Humiliation] is certainly hard to do well and feel
authentic, in control, and well received. I'm still
learning. When I get it right, it feels like magic.*

- LOVING DOM

THE PHRASE "HAPPY, HEALTHY HUMILIATION" may seem a contradiction to many. But it most definitely isn't. Happy and healthy is exactly how we want all participants to be at the end of the play. As we saw in the last chapter, there is a vast difference between someone who is being abusive and someone engaging in consensual, negotiated erotic kink play. But even if we take the potential for abuse off the table—if both parties exhibit affection, respect, and trust for one another and are truly focused on pleasure—it's not easy to achieve that ideal outcome. In this chapter, I'll share some of the obstacles to "happy, healthy humiliation," and then I'll show you how to overcome them through preparation, continuous consent, thorough aftercare, and problem-solving strategies for when something doesn't go as planned.

COMMON OBSTACLES TO MUTUALLY SATISFYING EROTIC HUMILIATION

Like any risky or "out-of-the-norm" activity, there are plenty of obstacles that might make it difficult for people to either find opportunities to engage or even express their interest in humiliation play. Here are a few that come up over and over again in my work:

NOT MANY PEOPLE FEEL COMFORTABLE OR KNOW HOW TO DO IT SAFELY

It's relatively easy to learn about and become comfortable with other types of kink, such as bondage or impact play, because there is so much easily accessible information about those interests. However, when it comes to erotic humiliation, the lack of reputable resources makes it much more difficult for potential players to educate themselves. And with so little information out there, it's difficult to build up the confidence you need to feel safe exploring humiliation. (That is, until you found this book!)

THERE'S A LOT OF JUDGMENT ABOUT IT, EVEN IN THE KINK WORLD

The stereotypes we discussed earlier lead to a lot of judgment about erotic humiliation, even from people who engage in pretty extreme forms of physical play. While, for many people, it's perfectly reasonable to want to be spanked or to tie somebody up, it's much more difficult to understand emotional masochism.

SUSPENSION OF DISBELIEF CAN BE DIFFICULT

Even people who harbor no judgments against erotic humiliation can find it difficult to overcome the cognitive dissonance around debasing someone they respect (or allowing someone they respect to treat them that way). This is particularly difficult for long-term, loving relationships. It isn't easy to call your spouse a loser!

TROUBLE SHIFTING FROM "REAL WORLD" MIND TO KINK MIND

One common struggle players encounter, no matter how experienced they are, is difficulty shifting into the mindset of erotic humiliation. One way I've found to overcome this is to **Pavlov yourself**. We all know Pavlov, right? He trained dogs to salivate when a bell rang by feeding them and ringing the bell simultaneously. Properly trained, the dogs would then salivate when the bell rang, even if there was no food presented. People are just like that. It's really handy. If you can start to associate naughty words and phrases or specific smells, objects, or even tastes with the feelings you're looking to bring up in humiliation play, then those **sensory sparks** can help you make the leap into the right mindset. Players can use sensory sparks to Pavlov themselves, and doms can also use them to get their subs in the mood.

IT'S HARD TO KNOW HOW TO DESCRIBE DESIRES

Our vocabularies are, frankly, pretty limited when it comes to describing the specific feelings we want to get from our humiliation scenes. After all, we're using negative words to describe our desires, and the language wasn't really built for that. Of course, it gets easier with practice, but it can be really difficult for someone who's just starting out to verbalize that nuance between "good" emotional pain and "bad" emotional pain.

PARTNERS OFTEN HAVE MISMATCHED LEVELS OF INTEREST

In existing relationships, it's not uncommon for one partner to be interested in erotic humiliation while the other is...less so. This disinterest could range from ambivalence ("That's not my jam, but I'm willing to try it for you") to absolute disgust. This mismatched interest can make it difficult, or even impossible, for the interested player to enact their desires (or even to express them to their partner).

All of these obstacles, combined with the negative stereotypes around erotic humiliation, can make it really hard for kinksters to get their erotic humiliation needs met. Often, they seem so imposing that would-be players find themselves wishing they *didn't* want what they want at all. This goes for both dominants and submissives. We often talk, in the kink world, about how much trouble subs have finding someone to treat them the way they want to be treated, but it's often even more difficult for a dominant person to admit to someone (especially to someone they know and respect) that they actively want to humiliate them.

Difficult, but not impossible! The obstacles may seem steep, but don't despair—once you know a little more about creating a mutually satisfying experience for yourself and your partner, your humiliation goals will start to seem much more achievable.

CREATING A POSITIVE EXPERIENCE FOR BOTH PARTNERS

Now that we understand the primary obstacles to embracing erotic humiliation, let's take a look at some best practices— for before, during, and after a scene—that will help overcome those obstacles and ensure everyone leaves satisfied.

CONSENT

As I mentioned in the previous chapter, consent is critical to any intimate encounter, including erotic humiliation. So let's take a deeper look at what it means to ask for and give consent. Consent, simply, is permission for something to happen. This permission must be given freely, enthusiastically, verbally, and continuously. Additionally, every party—regardless of gender, orientation, or role in play—is responsible for giving and asking for consent from their partners. Not only is this required as part of a healthy, happy experience, but it's also the law. Engaging in sexual activities without your partner's clear and ongoing consent is considered assault.

Informed consent is the most critical kind of consent. Everyone must know and understand what they're agreeing to, but there are several factors that may make that difficult or even impossible, inhibiting someone's ability to give consent. Here are some of the common ones to look out for:

- **Drugs, alcohol, medication, or exhaustion:** If someone is heavily under the influence, they may not be able to think clearly and critically enough to give informed consent.

- **Lack of experience:** Someone who is new to kink, or specifically to erotic humiliation, may not fully understand what they're consenting to. As the person asking for consent, it's your responsibility to be sure your partner knows what they're consenting to. As the person giving consent, if you're not sure you understand, it's your responsibility to ask for clarification.

- **"Newthusiasm" or overconfidence:** New players are often eager to try anything and everything, which translates to a confidence they haven't quite earned. But experienced players, too, can get cocky and find themselves in over their heads.

- **Competition:** Whether someone is trying to compete with another player (one dom "out-domming another," for example) or with themselves, if they're in the mindset of one-upmanship, they cannot give clear consent.

- **Relationship status or community standing:** There's often an implicit coerciveness that comes from another player's status or community stand-ing—a sense of, "Well, you're really important, so you must know what's right." Unfortunately, cer-tain leaders in the kink world have taken advan-tage of this, using status to justify not taking no for an answer. No matter who you're playing with—no matter how respected or high-status they are in the kink community or any other—you *never* have to agree to anything you don't want to do. And the reverse is also true: nobody should ever use their own status (or threaten yours) in order to coerce you into consenting.

- **Being in "top space" or "sub space":** When a scene is going really well, there's a mental shift that happens, sending you into a totally different headspace. If you're a dominant, your feelings of power can take over and cloud your judgment. If you're a sub, you may find yourself too deep in that headspace to fully consider what you do and don't want. When you're both in that headspace where you're feeling great about what's happen-ing, whether **sub space** or **top space**, it's a little bit like being just drunk enough to think two more shots sound like a great idea. But just like you're likely to regret those two shots the next morning, it can be too easy to blow past boundaries and pop that kink "bubble" when your logical brain has taken the afternoon off.

If you feel yourself in any of these situations—or if you see signs that your partner may be struggling to give informed consent for any reason—it may be time to press pause. And remember that consent isn't permanent, either. Even if you've already given your consent, you are free to revoke it at any time, for any reason. In more mainstream, **vanilla** encounters, all that's needed is "no" or "stop," but in kink encounters, it can be a little more complicated than that, as (consensual) force and struggling are often part of the fun. So, when you want to withdraw consent, be *very* clear. Do not just say no. Say, "I do *not* consent to this," or "I don't want this; you don't have my consent." In the BDSM world, the classic way to withdraw consent is by using a safeword. Again, "no" is *not* a good safeword. Pick something that you can *remember and say,* even in alternate headspaces, and agree on it with your partner before play begins. (If speech is restricted, use a safe gesture instead.)

To sum it up, to keep your play consensual, always remember these six things:

1. Consent is the responsibility of *all* parties. Give/remove your consent clearly, and always ensure the consent of your partner.

2. Consent doesn't have to be sexy to be important.

3. *Any* player can withdraw consent at *any* time for *any* reason. Everyone should have a safeword and a safe gesture.

4. Identify and communicate *your* wants, needs, and limits.

5. "Forced" refers to consensual non-consent. While the energy of the scene is that the person is being "forced" so they can experience giving up responsibility for what is happening to them, they must give consent before the scene begins and can withdraw it at any time.

6. If what you're hearing from your partner—or what you're saying, yourself—is "maybe," then the answer is no.

KINK-SPECIFIC CONSENT

Kinksters have different ways of talking about consent and kink, using these acronyms to describe various levels of risk within a scene:

R.A.C.K.

For many years the phrase "Safe, Sane, and Consensual" (**SSC**) was the most popular motto used to characterize careful kink, but recently people have started to more frequently use **R.A.C.K**.

R.A.C.K. stands for Risk Aware Consensual Kink, which is a safety motto in the kink community that is growing in popularity. It is a reminder to stay aware of the risks, both physical and psychological, that come with any level of not just kink, but any sexual interaction. Though R.A.C.K is a bit limiting in that it focuses primarily on awareness and not on active consent, I do prefer this framework to SSC because the concept of sanity comes with a lot of baggage. It implies a lot of judgment, and it's an incredibly subjective term. One person's "sane" is another person's "dangerous." Some risk will always be involved, so being aware of that risk within the framework of informed consent is more realistic.

P.R.I.C.K

Personal Responsibility in Consensual Kink (**P.R.I.C.K.**) is the only framework that specifically advocates for both parties (yes, subs, too) to take *active* roles in advocating and managing consent. Kink is certainly a team sport, and it's important for every person in a scene to look out, but each person has a responsibility to themselves and anyone else involved to bring their best game, which includes communicating desires, needs, and limits.

RELATIONSHIPS

As you prepare to engage in erotic humiliation, it's important to recognize that the relationship you have with the person you're playing with profoundly affects how a humiliation scene transpires. As with any BDSM activity, erotic humiliation is likely to look very different between partners engaging in pickup play, casual partners, and partners who are in committed, long-term relationships.

PICKUP PLAY

Pickup play is when you meet someone (for example at a play party or **munch**, or even online) and just dive right into the actual kink without much discussion beforehand. There are several pros to this kind of play. First, it's much easier to suspend your disbelief with a relative stranger than it is with someone you know. Additionally, if you're finding it's difficult to get your needs met within your own community, pickup play may be your best bet for finding someone whose interest in erotic humiliation matches your own. I meet a lot of kinky people, and I've found the number of requests for humiliation in pickup play can be fairly high, especially if you're a dominant willing to do any kind of humiliation work.

However, there are also plenty of cons to playing with people you don't know well, and humiliation play is not something you should just launch into without some preparation, because you never know where hot buttons, land mines, and triggers might lie. In fact, I don't do pickup play with humiliation anymore, because there are too many unknown hazards. This is deeply subtle psychological domination work and there's too much responsibility involved for me to feel comfortable navigating through all of the potential land mines.

It is a bad idea to meet somebody new in a dungeon and suddenly rip into their childhood trauma. (Though for some, the elevated risk adds to the fun.) Even if you have a negotiation with someone new and you ask, "What do you find humiliating?" they're not likely to answer with the same honesty, complexity, and nuance as someone with whom you have already built other layers of trust. This is particularly true when dealing with people who don't have a lot of experience, and quite frankly, that's most people. If, on the other hand, somebody comes to you and says, "I've been doing humiliation play for a decade. I've done all these specific things," there may be a little bit more wiggle room.

It's fascinating to me that people will put their physical bodies—not to mention their emotions—in the hands of people that they've just met. I have a lot of caution about pickup play in general. It's one of the reasons that I stopped offering professional sessions. If you're going to do psychological pickup play, please understand that it's absolutely critical to take some time to talk about hot buttons (more about that later in the chapter) and stick with lighter and less intense play to get started.

Heavy humiliation requires an element of trust that can only develop over time, so I enjoy it most (and can go the furthest) with subs I play with frequently. I prefer it lighter with casual playmates.

- J.V. Altharas

LONG-TERM RELATIONSHIPS

The reason I recommend engaging in erotic humiliation with someone you know at least a little bit—even if they're not your life partner—is that part of the process that makes it great is getting to know the person you play with. This trust and comfort lead to better, safer play. When I was building a relationship with a humiliation client, for example, I'd really look out for real-life instances in which they might be a little bit embarrassed so I could begin to eroticize those experiences for them.

Trust is also a significant factor when it comes to humiliation play. When there's a commitment between players that goes beyond the short-term scene and into long-term love and care, then each psychological torment scene becomes an exuberantly undertaken trust fall.

My desire for erotic humiliation has intensified over time. My desire is stronger now than ever because I belong to a Master who I trust completely. I was insecure in previous relationships and I struggled to compartmentalize humiliation in the context of a scene—I carried the shame with me well after the scene ended, questioning whether the person doing the humiliating really thought of me in such a way. With my Master, I am able to experience the thrill of being humiliated and the release that comes with it because I know He truly loves me and cares for me and He humiliates me for our mutual pleasure.

- Ashley Rose

On the opposite end of the spectrum from pickup play, erotic humiliation can be tricky for players in long-term, committed relationships, too. As a professional dominatrix for many years, I found that couples who were very kinky in their personal lives and explored lots of kink in their relationships would, at times, have to send their partners to pros to engage in humiliation. They have an advantage over pickup players because they know their partners—and their preferences, traumas, and triggers—so intimately. But, as I've mentioned, that very advantage can also backfire, because it can be hard to say, "I love you. You're the partner I commit to for the rest of my life. I am devoted to you. Now lick that trash can, you perverted loser!"

Ideally, it's a balance. You have to know someone well enough to know—or at the very least be good at getting them to reveal—what makes them uncomfortable, self-conscious, and embarrassed. And you need to know and trust someone well to be able to probe and then accurately read reactions and go deeper...and also to know when to slow down or back off so you don't cause lasting emotional harm. On the other hand, you have to be able to separate that very real affection from the less-than-affectionate behavior involved in humiliation play.

NO MATTER THE RELATIONSHIP, ALL PLAYERS HAVE THREE RESPONSIBILITIES

Whether you and your play partners met five minutes ago or have been playing together for thirty years, there are two things every party must commit to doing (once consent has been established) for erotic humiliation to work:

1. COMMUNICATE CLEARLY

Communication is 100 percent required for mutually satisfying, healthy erotic humiliation. We'll talk more about what, exactly, needs to be discussed in the upcoming negotiation chapter, but for now, it's important to internalize the value of clear, specific communication with your partner. This includes being as nuanced as possible when you're talking about feelings, triggers, desires, landmines, and even the particular language that can and can't be used in scene. After all, so many things come into play when using words: recent and historical context, local slang, community appropriation, and individual perception. We can choose to recontextualize or appropriate language in order to create a personal lexicon. Once we have our own lexicon, it's then important to see how it can sync up with play partners', lovers', and even friends'. We will discuss erotic, powerful, and taboo words and what they mean to us, and to the world around us.

> In all of the times we have played, she has only said it a couple of times but the first time she called me "Sissy" I reacted strongly, suddenly feeling quite insecure. It didn't stop play and if anything it pushed me deeper, but it was a word I wasn't ready for (despite

the barrage of humiliation I'd been receiving for an hour or so). I feel I am a strong male who submits, so this word made me wonder if she thought I was too feminine for her. She doesn't, we're fine, but it's amazing how much power a word or two can have.

- P

Communication doesn't stop when the scene begins, either. It is *always* both parties' responsibility to communicate when something doesn't feel right or needs to change. We'll talk about **safewords** and other verbal **shortcuts** later, but there are other ways to communicate clearly and freely without breaking scene, too. For example, I like to use **stage whispers** to check in with my submissives and empower them to give me feedback as needed mid-scene. Before play begins, I always remind my partners that, if you're whispering, it doesn't count as part of the scene, so they don't have to worry about "ruining it" when they express their needs. For example, one time I commanded a submissive to crawl on his knees, and as he started to crawl, I noticed a look of pain (not the good kind) flash across his face. So, in a stage whisper, I asked, "Is there something wrong with your knees?" And he stage-whispered back, "Yeah, they're hurting today." So, without missing a beat, I was able to put my dom voice back on and say, "I've changed my mind! Stop crawling and lie before me!" The scene went on, and my sub didn't destroy his knees. A win for everybody.

Tips and tricks aside, the most important thing to know is that communication is *never* going to ruin things. It may delay them, sure, but in the end, expressing your needs is only going to make things better.

2. ENSURE SAFETY

The second responsibility all players have is to look out for their own safety as well as their partners'. A lot of this, of course, is linked to communication: If you're tied up and your hands are going numb, it's your responsibility to speak up for your own safety. If you have a mental or physical health condition, say so before play begins so you and your partner can devise a scene that's both satisfying *and* safe—don't just keep it quiet out of fear your request to play will be denied. Communicate directly about STIs so that you and your partner can make educated decisions for everyone's health.

In scene, both players need to keep an eye on each other's safety by gauging each other's emotional space and being careful not to push boundaries. (Subs are responsible for this, too! Subs often don't feel like they can check in with their doms without breaking the power structure, but as a dom, I'm here to tell you that if my sub notices me getting triggered in a scene, I absolutely want them to use that safe word and check in.)

Outside of communication, safety involves logistics like keeping toys clean and sticking to safer sex practices, but it also means knowing when to keep certain elements *out* of a scene. In other words, part of safety is recognizing that some fantasies belong in our heads, either because our partner's have established limits around them or because bringing them to life would put us at real risk. (We'll dig into this more later in the chapter.)

3. CONTRIBUTE CREATIVELY

There's a mistaken belief that if a submissive tells a dominant what they want, what their fantasies are, or the fabulously perverted ideas they've been brainstorming, that that's trying to take control of the scene (sometimes it's called "topping from the bottom" which I talk about later in the book). In reality, each player should be contributing creatively to the scene so that it ends up being satisfying and successful for everybody.

> *I think that I'm more open to trying new things now, and I've really enjoyed them. I came into humiliation with only my own fantasies to go on, but you meet other people and see their fantasies and those will rub off on you. I think that my hard limits will remain hard, but I'm definitely interested in trying a lot of things.*
>
> *- Foot Rest Boy*

With all of that in mind, here are some steps to get you started.

GETTING STARTED

BRINGING IT UP

Whether you're seeking a new partner with whom to explore your erotic humiliation desires or you'd like to introduce erotic humiliation into your current relationship, broaching the subject can feel almost as intimidating as the play itself.

> *I think the biggest obstacle is explaining the fetish to partners. I've only confessed my submissive fantasies and I've only indulged my partners in their submissive fantasies. It's hard to say, "I want to collar you and write 'slut' on your forehead," to someone you love and respect.*
>
> *- Foot Rest Boy*

I'm often asked for recommendations for how humiliation lovers can meet people who share their interests. I understand it can be hard, but luckily we live in an age of many options for connections. Websites, social media, and in-person events are all possibilities, it's just a matter of putting yourself out there. My strongest suggestion on meeting someone with your interests is to actually *share* those interests. Maybe don't introduce yourself with it. "Hi, my name is Bob, and I want you to stuff me into a trashcan," is not likely to get you a lot of dates. Neither does, "Hello, I'm Goddess Susan, and I love to spit on people while I make them sit in pies." But, being honest about your desires and the type of player you're looking for is much more likely to land you the kinkster of your dreams.

> *Bringing it up is always hard. i get very embarrassed expressing any humiliation i'd like to experience, because it usually involves talking about deeply personal experiences. Building that kind of trust that i find i need also takes time.*
>
> *- Erin Quinn*

Similarly, if you're interested in introducing erotic humiliation into your relationship with a current significant other—whether you've been together a few weeks, a few months, or several years—the best way to start is by being honest about your desires. I know it can be intimidating to bring it up with both strangers and long-term partners. Here are a few ideas to get you started:

- **Bring it up in a fictional context.** Read erotica or watch porn together and talk about what turns you on. Even less intimidating, look for examples of the kind of humiliation you're interested in in pop culture movies, and ask your partner if they'd ever be interested in trying something like that. (I promise you, there's fodder for erotic humliation all over pop culture—it's fairly innocuous in reality, like a food fight or some verbal teasing, but we transmute it into something sexual. I call it "covert porn for perverts." Don't believe me? Start with *Dazed and Confused*, and just try to tell me the seniors girls' hazing activities aren't inspirational.)

- **Create equivalency with more "normalized" acts.** Bring up physical acts you enjoy (whether they're kinky or vanilla) and tell your partner which psychological activities give you the same charge.

- **Get inspiration from games.** I love a good game of truth or dare or "have you ever" as an entrypoint for discussing new or "offbeat" desires. You can find lots of card decks for games like these online (including in my shop!), and they're a great way to find inspiration and start conversations.

- **Acknowledge the weirdness.** It's okay to start with, "I know it's strange, but…" or "I can't believe this turns me on, but…" If you're afraid expressing your interest outright might put your partner on the defensive, framing it with your own vulnerability can be a great way to kick off the conversation.

- **Use this book!** Read through it and highlight or dog-ear pages that will help your partner understand what you're asking for. You'll still need to share more about your personal experiences and desires, but this book can give you a jumping-off point for the conversation.

SETTING GOALS TOGETHER

Understanding what level you're each looking to play at is essential to making sure you're both on the same page. If you're looking for a little embarrassment play and your partner launches into full degradation, neither one of you will be pleased. Or, if you *are* looking for degradation and all they do is call you a slut, then no one is satisfied. Such a denial—and not the fun kind.

(The denial of the desired type of play can be really fun if it's done *conscientiously*, with both players understanding that that will be the game. But if it's not done on purpose, it just ends up being frustrating.)

Being sure you're on the same level, on the other hand, sets scenes for success. Talk about what you are looking to get out of the experience, and understand that it's easier and healthier for you to ramp up from a basic kind of experimental play into scenes of higher intensity. If you find you're short on ideas—whether you're a veteran player who feels stuck in a rut or a newbie who's just getting started—you can use negotiation lists, truth or dare decks, scene-planning workbooks, or other tools for inspiration. Check out the back of this book for a few recommended resources.

DISCUSSING LIMITATIONS AND TRIGGERS

A key part of goal setting is discussing your limitations—the boundaries you aren't willing to cross in a scene. Limitations are not a bad thing. Quite the opposite. Knowing each other's limitations actually gives you more freedom, because you can do what you're doing with as much confidence as possible within the predetermined parameters.

When engaging in humiliation play, there are no physical identifiers to look out for to know if something is going in a negative direction—another reason it's so critical to discuss these limits and **triggers** (or **hot buttons**) thoroughly before play begins. If you're spanking somebody or tying somebody up, there are physical elements to look for: the reddening of skin, the blue flesh coloration if they're losing oxygen. But when you're doing psychological play, it's different. You can be fine, safe, having a great time, and then all of a sudden: Bam! *Holy fuck*, what just happened?

LIMITATIONS YOU AND YOUR PARTNER MIGHT DISCUSS

When it comes to discussing limits and triggers, nothing is, well, off-limits. These are a few categories it's important to touch on, but you can (and should) add anything else you'd like.

- **Physical boundaries:** Any chronic pain or sensory issues can create limits. For example, if one partner has back problems, they may not be able to sustain hunched positions, and that's something to discuss before play begins.

- **Mental health boundaries:** These may include topics or words that are off-limits (body image is a big one for many players), or it may include frequent pre-scene discussions about both partners' mental states. Acute bouts of depression or anxiety, for example, can bring triggers closer to the surface and require stricter limits than usual.

- **Past traumas:** Everyone, not just subs, can have previous traumatic experiences (verbal abuse, assault, etc.) that lead to limits in humiliation play.

- **Words that aren't acceptable:** Words can be triggering for people in very specific ways. A perfectly acceptable concept, described in different words, can hit a player completely differently. Someone who loves being called a slut, for example, may shut down when called a skank. (Words may not be the only communication-related limitation to consider. Raised voices or even whispers may be triggering to some players.)

- **Mentioning other people in play:** Maybe your partner has a hard limit on bringing up their family during scenes (e.g., "Your mother was never proud of you"), or maybe you don't want to mention non-consenting individuals (e.g. "I want you to jerk-off with your wife's underwear), or maybe there are whole groups or categories of people one of you would prefer to leave out.

- **Any ongoing, sensitive issues:** Whether these issues are in your relationship with your partner or elsewhere in your life, you should consider adding anything you're currently dealing with to the limitations list. If you're mad at your partner for never folding the laundry, it might be okay to bring that into the scene, but more often, anything that you are actually upset or angry about should be discussed seriously rather than invoked in play. Those issues will create a different tone in your voice and body and are likely to edge away from "good pain" territory. In my opinion, it's best to stick to things that don't have emotional attachment or things that have already been worked through.

UNEXPECTED LIMITATIONS: MAKING ADJUSTMENTS MID-SCENE

Discussing limitations ahead of time is absolutely critical. That said, it's important to understand that unexpected issues might come up in the process of playing, particularly if you're both new to exploring this kind of interaction. It's often said that you don't usually learn where boundaries are until someone crosses them. You can be in the middle of an intense scene with extreme physical sensation, when suddenly a gentle face slap will re-traumatize your sub; and the same is possible in an intense humiliation scene, where despite all the degradation involved, a moment of lighter teasing can trip an unexpected trigger. (Some kinksters *want* to explore

BDSM as a way of transforming a negative experience into a positive one by revisiting certain behaviors in a safe environment, but it's better for that to be a choice rather than an accident.)

It's important to talk about these landmines up front to the best of everyone's ability, but the idea that you can simply trust someone else to know what their limits are is a pernicious myth of the BDSM world that we desperately need to break. Our community breeds untruths and believes its own bullshit. I've had frustrating experiences with people that say, "Oh my god! Please beat me and leave me in the basement!" and then balk when I try to deliver the pain they've requested. Their response is, "Ow, that hurts! What are you doing?"

People similarly overestimate their desires to be humiliated and degraded, which is why starting small and ramping up is so vital to developing a healthy scene. Sometimes, someone is all gung ho about a particular fantasy, but for whatever reason, it doesn't work like they think it should in play. This may be because it's not something that can be done ethically, but more often it's because we realize as we get started that we don't actually *want* what we enjoy fantasizing about. (Rape and ravishment fantasies are common ones that people realize they don't actually want to play out, and these mid-scene discoveries can cause real confusion for both players.) We live in an "if you can dream it, you can (and should!) do it" culture, which often makes people feel like their fantasies "don't count" unless they play them out. In reality, sometimes the logistics of bringing a fantasy to life ruin the fun. (For example, did you ever notice that, in action movies, the hero never has to stop and take a shit? All those epic chases would be far less glamorous in real life.) Sometimes, our fantasies should remain just that. But sometimes, we don't realize that until we're already mid-scene. When that happens, it's perfectly okay to make adjustments.

> *I was bottoming once, which is a rare occasion, and my top wanted me to eat my own cum. I had been beaten, cut, fingered, fucked, but I had to draw the line there. I called red and ended the scene. We still laugh about it now because she thought everything else was much worse, but I just couldn't lower myself to do that.*
>
> *- I*

Finally, there's just plain-old human inconsistency. People can have a different response on Tuesday than they do on Friday to the exact same activity. It just depends on what has happened to them that day or that week, where they are emotionally, and where their hormones levels are currently. Though hormones and inconsistencies are generally— unfairly, patriarchally — attributed to those who identify as women, this is true across the gender spectrum. Hormones are the chemical encoders of desire and control the strongest urges of the body, like hunger, tiredness, fear, and sex. All of the body's complex and interconnected systems affect how you experience kinky play of any kind. In order to be a safe kinky person, you have to be okay with the fact that boundaries are, by nature, flexible and fallible.

GAUGING EACH OTHER'S LIMITS

Whether you're a dominant or a submissive, it's your responsibility to communicate your limits as clearly as you possibly can before play begins. (Yes, dominants can and do have limits, too!) And if something you hadn't recognized as a limit comes up within a scene, you have the right and responsibility to communicate that, too. Remember: consent is an ongoing conversation.

Both dominants and submissives must respect their partners' limits before and during a scene. If you're a submissive, you have to be careful not to ask your dominant not to do or say things they're uncomfortable with. If you're a dominant, you must continually gauge your submissive's responses for potential surprise limitations. Although you may be the center of the universe in the fantasy you've created and , your word may be law in the context of your roles in the scene, your submissive is human and may not respond to you the way you expect, or even in the way that they normally do. When this is the case, it's your responsibility to make adjustments.

You must also recognize that your partner may not realize their own limits, and may make requests that you know or suspect are beyond what they are prepared to endure. Sometimes you as the dominant will know your sub's limits before they do. Sometimes you'll detect this using your empathy; sometimes it's obvious in the submissive's body language.

> I had one personal submissive who was completely service-oriented and humiliation-oriented, but he also knew that I like to dish out consensual pain. So he tried. He said, "Please restrain me and beat me," and I indulged him on the request for restraint, even though I'm not super into bondage. I prefer the ongoing consent inherent in the submissive "staying still" for the action. But I tried it anyway. I bound him into place and introduced some very light impact play. He groaned and made frustrated,

not sexy noises. I could feel his anger building. He attempted this kind of activity even though it was majorly triggering for him and did not engage his desire.

When I told him I was going to stop, he cried out, disgusted with himself, "No! You are the princess; I am the slave. I will do it." I had to assert my dominance and steer him away from his own poorly perceived limits. "No, I am the princess, you are the slave; you will *not* do this."

By the way, subs aren't the only players who can have limits. The stereotypical expectation may be that dominants are always dominant, that we just always want to be in control of everything all the time. But the truth is that very few people actually live up to that. Even the most dominating dominants may have days when they just aren't feeling it, and that's okay. No matter what role you take on, allow yourself the freedom to say, "You know what? I just don't feel good doing that right now, and we need to wait."

That's R.A.C.K.

RAMPING UP

I've mentioned **ramping up** before, and it's worth a closer look now, because this is another really important part of humiliation. What is ramping up? Picture a ramp. It doesn't increase in sudden increments, like stairs. Instead, it moves smoothly upward, little by little. This lets you gauge your progress as you go and decide whether things are moving the way you had hoped. It gives you time to check in before you've gone too far.

Physical play features obvious signposts. For psychological play, there are no visual markers. If I'm wailing on you with a cane, welts will show up. I'm going to be able to see at least how your physical body is responding to my efforts. But if I'm unknowingly calling you the same name that your childhood bullies used to and causing you to freak out, there is no indication of your psychological response unless you share it with me voluntarily (or involuntarily). This isn't meant to scare you, but it's meant to make you understand that humiliation play is both subtle work and heavy-duty.

If you want to approach it in a healthy way, you're better off ramping up rather than diving in the deep end. The idea is not to jump in blindly and then have to find your way back to land if something goes wrong.

> *I fantasize about levels of humiliation that are way above what I have actually experienced, and I don't know if I would ever be willing to go to such extremes in reality.*
>
> *- M*

A great example of this is "forced" bisexual play. Oftentimes, when someone (in this case, a cis-gendered man) thinks they're ready for high-intensity play, they end up freaking out when they get exactly what they asked for. Instead of jumping straight to cocksucking.a real penis, I'd recommend this "ramping up" technique, which allows low- and no-pressure ways to explore the desire in a way that allows you to gauge whether everyone is genuinely ready for a higher intensity edge-play version of the scene.

Step 1. Start with face fucking with the dominant's fingers

Step 2. Make them do sexual mouth stretches

Step 3. Start oral sex practice on a fun-looking dildo

Step 4. Once comfort and skills are established, move on to a realistic looking dildo

Step 5. Finally, *maybe*, after there's been a long build-up and plenty of time to communicate, consider, and explore in no-pressure ways, *then* escalate the play to incorporating biocock. Maybe.

It's perfectly acceptable to keep some fantasies in your head or at a playful/theatrical level! A fantasy doesn't have to be enacted in real life for you to get a lot of pleasure out of it. In fact, sometimes it's actually better to keep some fantasies in the (nearly) perfectly controllable environment of your imagination.

> *During race play, when a racial slur [was used]... though it was asked for, it was triggering to a submissive. He called his safe word, we talked it through and discussed why that had triggered him, and tried to get to the root of why he had these desires and what they meant to him. And just knowing that sometimes having a fantasy is fine, but you may not [actually] want to live that out in real life.*
>
> *- Bella Vendetta*

> *I have a better understanding of the divide between what I like to fantasize about when I*

masturbate and what I enjoy experiencing with a partner in real life. Humiliation is present in both, but at different intensities. My masturbation fantasies are very dark and degrading, whereas the kinds of scenes I enjoy doing with my girlfriend are more rooted in humiliation as an expression of my submission to her. Learning to separate those things has been illuminating and freeing.

- cloquirk

Like most things, success begets success, so when people have experiences that feel good, they want to have more of those experiences. If you wade into the shallow end, trying out some name-calling and minor embarrassment, you can get feedback as to whether what you're doing is working and if it is good enough to proceed and gain intensity. If you jump in the deep end of degradation, stripping someone of their name or humanity right off the diving board without having much understanding or experience at shallower depths, then it's much harder to get back to where you both have your heads above water. Ramping up builds anticipation and gives you a safe set of steps before someone becomes lost in the lower-than-sheep-shit deep end.

With psychological play it's not always as easy to see the scars, but that doesn't mean they don't exist. Proceed with caution and care, use your safewords, and communicate!

KEEP IT SIMPLE

Just like starting in the emotional shallow end, I would encourage new kinksters to start in the logistical shallow end as well, letting themselves experiment with humiliation in its simplest forms before making things more complicated.

What do I mean by complicated? **Kink extravaganza** is a term I've coined for the expectations people have for the elaborate trappings, costumes, staging, and time that they think must be a part of a successful kinky encounter. Think of a kink extravaganza like a circus, with so many bells and whistles it's easy to lose track of the action. Regardless of whether you are new to the BDSM world or are a long-time kinkster, it's easy to get caught up in the idea of kink extravaganza. We want to have the time, privacy, and equipment to put together a full three-ring circus show, or it just doesn't seem worth it. If we're not going to do a three-hour bondage scene, where you're strapped to the ceiling fan with me turning it on and off, then what is the point? (That's something I've wanted to do forever! Someday, when I am filthy rich, I'm going to have a man-size ceiling fan built. Yes, I will take photos and videos and invite people over to enjoy the show.) But that kind of scene isn't always going to be possible. People have jobs and partners and kids and lives. Sometimes we can't go to the circus, but we can have a little sidewalk carnival or a weekend puppet show. We can work it out.

Find a timeframe that's not only attractive to you but works realistically within your lifestyle. Letting go of the circus act requirement can help you incorporate your kink more regularly into your life rather than feeling frustrated because you're waiting for some momentous, crazy time to be able to do ALLTHETHINGS. Through experience, we learn to take what time we have and say, "Okay, you know what? We've got an hour. Let's start from there."

AFTER THE SCENE

As I mentioned before, one of the key differences between ethical play and abuse is that, in ethical play, the players are committed to building each other back up at the end of a scene. When a scene goes well, this is called **aftercare**, and it's a celebration of success. When it goes poorly, when a trigger is hit, then the grieving player is cared for in a different way, using the **trigger plan**. I'll discuss each individually, because most of us need different things when we're celebrating than when we're grieving, but the structure of each is roughly the same.

Both your after care plans and your trigger plans will be built around one question: *How do you want to feel after the scene?* Maybe during the scene you wanted to feel used, but afterward you likely have a completely different goal feeling, whether that's cherished, celebrated, worshiped, or anything else. These after-scene plans will contain four elements that, if done right, will lead to your goal feelings.

1. **Environment**: Do you need particular music, sounds, or TV shows? Do you want lights on or off?

2. **Communication**: Do you want to talk about the scene (positive or negative) immediately, or do you want to schedule a time to discuss later so you can process on your own? (Always, *always* make time to discuss a scene, particularly if a trigger was tripped. But it's okay if that time isn't right after.)

3. **Objects**: Are there any specific personal items or foods you need after a scene?

4. **Actions**: Do you need to be cuddled, or do you need to run laps around the block to blow off steam?

If you're not sure what you're going to need, that's okay. This can be particularly difficult for new players, who may have difficulty imagining what they'll need—or how they'll want to feel—after a scene. Start by thinking about non-kink experiences, sexual or otherwise. When have you felt really good, and what did you need or crave then? What about other times when you've felt bad? What's built you back up? Then, imagine the added intensity that comes from the taboo nature of the kink experience. Do you envision yourself wanting *more* of the same treatment that you crave after a more "normal" experience, or something different? For example, if you love to hear words of affirmation after traditional sex, will the added layer of humiliation mean you need *more* words of affirmation (like a one-page essay on how great the scene was) or some other kind of engagement?

Also remember that neither aftercare needs nor trigger plans are written in stone. These can evolve over time, and they can even evolve in the moment. For example, maybe you were certain that, if triggered, you'd need your partner to make you hot chocolate and snuggle with you. But in the moment after a trigger occurs, all you want is to be by yourself or to go to the gym. That's okay! As they say, "The best laid plans of mice and perverts," right? What matters is that you and your partner make these plans beforehand so you have a jumping-off point to meet each other's needs, whatever happens, and then continuously communicate as those needs evolve.

AFTERCARE

Aftercare is an important part of any kind of kink scene, especially if you're playing with someone whom you care about or would like to play with again! Taking the time to "come down" together and either talk about the scene or just cuddle and be close to reaffirm your connection is a great way to process what has just happened between you.

Why? Because the thing that makes humiliation play healthy and happy is this underlying sense of affection and the fact that at some point, even though you may take somebody really low, they can trust that you're not going to leave them there. It's not about making someone lesser, shitting on them, and walking away. Instead, it's an ongoing process of BDSM play.

Taking someone to a very low place in a loving way can be a cathartic exercise for both participants, but a lot of the stuff that kinky people do looks pretty twisted on the surface. If I'm whipping someone with a single-tail whip, even with remarkable skill that would make kinksters say, "Ooh, ahh," I'm still whipping someone. That's a thing that you're not really supposed to do to people in this day and age, but it's okay in the kink world because there's this assumption that they're going to be cared for afterward. Humiliation play is no different from any of that. Engaging in behaviors that are considered rude or mean while accepting that, afterward, you will help each other return to your regularly scheduled programs, can help both individuals go further in BDSM and the self-knowledge it brings.

You may take somebody to the depths of what their psyche will withstand, but you both have to plan to come out of that as whole people afterward. While both parties should be full participants in aftercare, ultimately the dominant is responsible for creating a totally safe space, even while perhaps making the submissive *feel* incredibly unsafe. That's the magic of a mind fuck!

AFTERCARE IS FOR EVERYBODY

Submissives aren't the only ones who need aftercare. Though it may not be obvious, dominants can need aftercare, too. Knowing that they aren't bad people for wanting to do such horrible things is key to maintaining the confidence they need to keep doing the naughty things that you both desire.

There is a persistent and yet absolutely false opinion that you are less domly if you need to be reassured that what you're doing is appreciated. I don't mean appreciation just in the form of groveling, although that can be fun, and I encourage it in my submissives! I mean appreciation in the form of submissives letting dominants know that they recognize the taboos that we struggle with to do what we do and are grateful that we do it. To think that dominants don't struggle at all with what we do would be an incorrect assumption.

Again, human first, dominant second.

As a top I have found it is imperative that I have aftercare after humiliation scenes. I really need to debrief and share some neutral, caring energy with my bottom afterward to know that what I've just done was okay and make sure they are feeling whole and safe—and to make sure my brain knows that what we just did together was consensual, intentional, and not wrong or dirty (even if it was a little dirty). I get dom drop without it.

- Zoey Belladonna

Whichever side of the dynamic you are on, let your partner know what they can do for aftercare, in whatever way is appropriate. Maybe you'd like them to bring you a glass of water or a cup of coffee. Perhaps you'd like to be thanked or have your feet kissed. It doesn't matter what the action is, but give yourself space to figure it out, because that's also part of responsible humiliation. How in the world can you take care of (or do gnarly, awesome things to) somebody else, or have gnarly, awesome things done to you, if you are not taking care of yourself? It's the circle of responsibility. Like the in-flight safety card says: put on your own mask before helping others.

A NOTE ABOUT AFTERCARE IN PROFESSIONAL SCENES

When you see a professional dominatrix or other sex worker, it's especially important to think about and communicate your aftercare needs so that you don't run out of time. Of course, any submissive who needs aftercare should be able to negotiate to receive it, but that time needs to be budgeted into your session. There's a similarity to working with a psychologist: even if the session gets intense, when the time is up, the time is up. An ethical professional won't let you be a danger to yourself, but keep your expectations appropriate to the dynamic.

ONGOING AFTERCARE

Though immediate aftercare is often critical for both players, I've found that a particular need for aftercare in humiliation play especially centers around the "drop" that happens anywhere from hours to days later. These activities can be confusing, even for experienced kinksters. Questions such as, "Why do I want to do this?" or "How could I let someone do those things to me?" are common and should be addressed. These feelings of **sub drop** and **top drop** are very real and may affect your ability to continue playing if they aren't respectfully considered. Most people have spent their lives learning that this sort of interaction is wrong, so it can be tough to unlearn that.

If and when this kind of drop happens, there are a few ways to deal with it. Having each person communicate their affection, acceptance, and appreciation is a good start. Knowing that you can talk to each other (or to a designated surrogate) is important to the processing of your experiences. Reassurance from all players that the action was desired and enjoyed can be a good way to counteract the socialization that we shouldn't be doing "this sort of thing."

PROCESSING YOUR EXPERIENCES

Contrary to popular belief, not everyone needs traditional aftercare. If you're someone, either dominant or submissive, who doesn't feel the need for snuggle time or conversation, this doesn't make you "wrong." But even if that's the case, it's necessary to discuss this with your partner so that you both know what each other may or may not need.

> *I prefer to relate to a Dom as always a Dom. Overt aftercare is too much like equalising our statuses and can spoil the relationship. My self-care afterwards is to go home, review in my mind, and enjoy the recollections.*
>
> *- Matthew*

I think aftercare might spoil the humiliation aspect. Hugs and cuddles and talking happen anyway during a relationship, but aftercare would spoil it for me. I like to be left in the humiliated state.

- squeezed_melon

Even if you don't need or want "typical" aftercare, it's important to spend some time, both individually and together, processing what worked and what didn't work in the scene. You can use a paper or digital journal (like *Scene Notes*, which you'll find on the reference page in the back of this book) to make notes about things you did that you'd like to build upon, things you'd like to pursue, or things you really didn't like or that didn't work like you thought they would. After you reflect individually—or right away if you'd prefer—you can talk in person or online about what the scene was like for each of you.

And here's some fun news: you can absolutely frame this post-play communication within your power dynamic, if you so desire. For example, I find one fun approach is to have the submissive write a thank you note to describe how the scene was for them. Additionally, you can make custody of the reflection journal both a responsibility and a joy. Get creative with it! Does the sub have to conceal it or carry it ostentatiously? Are they in trouble if they stain it with coffee? Do they have to send you pictures of where they keep it near their bed?

WHEN THINGS GO AWRY

For years, I watched people discuss aftercare as if it was for both winding down great scenes and recovering from mishaps. That always rubbed me the wrong way, because those two scenarios are not the same. Finally, I realized we needed a different way to talk about what happens when things go wrong. Because when it comes to this kind of play, the question is not *whether* something will go wrong, but *when*. If a dominant accidentally hits a trigger, it's not the end of the world—and it may not even have to be the end of the scene (though it's ok if it is). But it *does* require some response and care to acknowledge the incident and protect both the submissive and the dominant from risk of a full breakdown. This will look very different from aftercare that follows a successful scene. In a responsible kink relationship, you and your partner would discuss this eventuality *before* starting play. To help make that discussion more concrete and ensure everyone—and particularly the dominant—knows what to do when something goes wrong, I've created a concept called the **trigger plan.**

The big question you're hoping to answer with a trigger plan is, "If something goes wrong, what do we do next?"

When you negotiate a humiliation scene you must ask, "If we hit an emotional trigger for you, what do you think you would need? Do you need me to dismiss you and give you space to work it out? Do you need me to hug you? Even if that may or may not be part of our dynamic?" Some people need or want to be pushed through. If that's the case, it's the submissive's responsibility to clearly say, "If I start crying, please push me through."

Other subs may need the dom to de-escalate. You may need to work together to negotiate what kind of physical or emotional state is required to make the sub feel safe. If you're a dominant, you must also consider your own feelings and limits; have you ever acted this way before? How will you feel knowing that you've (accidentally) put your submissive in this kind of pain while staring it in the face?

Figuring out what the best possible next step is for both of you after hitting a negative trigger is time well-invested. Creating a trigger plan may not sound sexy, but I'm a fan of practical kink because it tends to be more successful kink, which means you'll do it more often and it'll be more fun!

> *The first time he came on my face it brought up a lot of baggage I didn't know I had. He went into Daddy mode and cleaned me up and held me while I cried, and we picked apart where the "processing error" was that triggered my extreme reaction. (We routinely do that kind of developmental post-mortem on our play.) We decided that he would "threaten" me with it during future play, and when I felt ready to try again I would give him a predetermined cue. It went much better the next time.*
>
> *- Corrine*

If you've been playing together for a long time, it's still helpful to quickly remind yourselves of any trigger plans right before you do a humiliation scene.

APOLOGIES AND BLAME

Nobody is perfect, even with preparation. Understand that no matter how long you have known somebody, you can still hit emotional landmines. Remember what I said about every day being different? When you do hit that landmine, part of having your trigger plan ready is keeping two things in mind:

1. Blame is not helpful in either direction. Submissives may blame the dominant, assuming that a truly responsible dominant would never do anything wrong. Similarly, dominants may subscribe to the stereotypical notion that "it's always the submissive's fault" (which can be a fun part of play but falls apart when real life creeps in). In either case, both parties should reexamine and discuss those beliefs.

2. Apologies are not only acceptable from dominants, but sometimes they're necessary. With my submissives, I never break the D/s dynamic, but have I ever apologized for screwing up? Absolutely! That doesn't take away any "domliness." I've never broken any hard limits, but whenever I have screwed up and maybe gone a little bit further than intended or said something too intense, I've stopped and said, "You know what? I'm really sorry. That was not my intention. Where can we take the scene to make sure that we keep this in proper headspace?"

Even as a dominant, don't be afraid to say, "I didn't anticipate that. I'm sorry."

Everybody screws up, because we're human, and humans make mistakes. That said, there are different levels of screw-up, and each should be handled differently:

- **An unexpected reaction to a consensual word or activity**: This really isn't a screw-up, and it's nobody's fault. It's still a trigger, so it needs to be treated as such, but rather than categorize it as a mistake, consider it new data for the next round of pre-scene negotiations.

- **A clear screw-up:** If you told me not to spit on you, but I got caught up in the moment and did, that's my mistake, and I owe you a sincere apology. But if we move straight into the trigger plan and work together to help you overcome it without spinning our wheels rehashing the issue, then we should be able to move forward and play together in the future. (In these situations, remember two things: first, there's a difference between processing and just stirring shit up, and second, that sometimes the triggered partner will need to process with someone other than the person who triggered them.)

- **Willful abuse of power:** If a player intentionally blows past a limit, either because they're disregarding the other's wishes or because they're a dominant who assumes the language or actions that are off-limits will be the most humiliating, then this isn't a screw-up but a willful abuse of power. The triggered partner should stop play immediately and think very carefully before agreeing to engage with this person again.

As long as you are doing the best you can to be ethical, to do things in a consensual manner, and to make sure that there is a strong foundation of affection at the very least, if not love, for the person you're playing with, then you are playing in a risk-aware way. Understand that triggers will get pulled, that you (the dominant) might feel bad occasionally, and that they (the submissive) might feel bad occasionally; the important part is how you deal with it and how you move forward through it.

When a trigger is tripped, I deal with it by doing whatever was negotiated for that person prior to play beginning. Main thing is, I switch off humiliation words, tone, stance, activity and move to that of a carer. Still dominant and so in control, but lovely and human and caring.

- Mistress Lux

WAYS TO HELP SUBMISSIVES GET THROUGH TOUGH EXPERIENCES

If a scene crashes and burns, that doesn't have to be the end of all your fun forever. There is always something to be learned from "failure," and there are even ways to make it part of the domination. One of the things that you can do to incorporate it into the scene is to declare the submissive an utter failure and give them another assignment. Or if you give a sub an assignment and they're just not doing it, you can decide to talk about it at a later date and shift gears.

You can use the fact that they couldn't follow through to create a sense of humiliation. Give them another task that you feel more certain about, or that is more familiar, and then try to figure out later what went wrong. A tip that I've come to rely on to get around reluctance to discuss limits and failures is written confession. You can assign your sub a journal or a confession book of emails where they explain their transgressions and why they did not perform to your orders. Once they let go of grammar and spelling concerns, many people are generally better in this format than they are face-to-face. This is a great way to find out what people are afraid to talk about.

You can also offer another option—a worse option—as an alternative to the activity that they're struggling with. This is not a very nurturing approach, but it is a technique you can use to get somebody through if you know them well.

Which leads me to the toilet-licking story.

> I had a guy who offered to buy me a brand-new toilet, set it in the living room, and have me order him to lick it. What fun is that? Loser! The whole point is that you don't know if the toilet has been cleaned or not before I make you lick it. (I'm super squeamish, so I always had it cleaned. (I don't want to watch you lick a dirty toilet. That's disgusting. If I dry heave that's not supportive of my dominant power.) I would have a different submissive come in and clean the toilet, then wipe it down with water so it didn't smell like cleaning agent. Then I would threaten to make the other, first submissive lick the toilet. If he couldn't bring himself to lick the toilet, I would supply worse-sounding alternatives in order to raise the stakes. "If you can't lick the toilet, I'm going to make you go outside and get a spoonful of dirt and swallow it."

When I'm feeling a bit more gentle, I use another technique where I lend them my strength as the dominant. Remember, they want to submit to your desires, but they have all of their own struggles, whether they like it or not.

When this happens, I get to share my confidence in them and say, "I know you can do this. I know you can. You're going to take a deep breath and you're going to do it. You're going to lick that toilet! You're going to lick it! You're going to love it!" I high-five my submissives. I cheer them on. "Yay, bitch! You licked the toilet! Score one for you!"

I've found that eye contact is one of the most effective motivators. What I would often do is make someone look me into my eyes—locked in eye contact—and emphatically say, "I know you can do this. I know you can. Are you going to doubt me? Do you doubt me and my assessment of your abilities? No!"

There's also the simple device of rewards. People love bribes. We're all four-year-olds who want a cookie. Everyone! It's important, of course, that you use a reward that means something. It wouldn't have been very motivating if I was offering something that wasn't special. For example, at the end of every session, my submissives got to say goodbye to me by kissing my feet, so since they were going to get to do that anyway, it wouldn't have been a good reward. It's important to really make that reward part of the experience, worth suffering through something truly horrible in order to get it. I've found that those two things—lending my strength in a nurturing way and bribing people—are excellent options.

WHAT TO DO AFTER A TRIGGER HAS BEEN TRIPPED

Sometimes, if a really difficult trigger has been tripped, getting back on track isn't as simple as finding an alternative. When that happens, then what?

Once a trigger has been hit, the first step is to assess what the triggered partner needs. In this scenario, it's best just to be clear and direct. If you're a dominant, it may seem scary to stop the scene and lose your power, but if you blunder forward, you're going to ruin your scene anyway—and you may ruin your sub in the process. So err on the side of ruining the scene with communication and caution rather than trauma. You can use the stage whispers I talked about before, or you can just pump the brakes and pull out of the scene. Either way, go ahead and ask your partner, "Do you need to stop?"

> I'm a minefield. I've handled [triggers being tripped] any way from being told to suck it up (in well established M/s relationships) to stopping the scene to talk, to simply moving on to something else. All of them have worked and all of them have also blown up.
>
> - Scarlet Begonias

If they say no, then you can proceed with the scene, but I recommend downshifting the intensity and/or changing your activity when you do. As a dominant, I'll narrate what I'm doing and what I want my sub to do so they don't have to grasp for what's going on while they're trying to figure out how they feel. I'll say, "I'm going to continue the play now. You're going to do such and such if you need me to take another break." Then I continue the scene, giving them straight, easy-to-follow instructions.

If the triggered partner says they do need to stop, then stop the play immediately and switch to the trigger plan. At this point, the scene is over, and my personal recommendation is not to resume play the same day, even after working through the trigger plan. If you do, however, start a completely different scene and at a much lower intensity level to give yourselves time and space to get back into your rhythm, rebuilding both tension and trust before you ramp it back up.

The bottom line to avoid letting things go awry—or to fix them when they do—is to be sure you don't get so caught up in bringing your fantasies to life that you disregard the ramifications of unsafe play in reality.

CHAPTER 5

NEGOTIATION AND COMMUNICATION FOR HUMILIATION

I've also found that my communication skills have grown ten-fold. It's easy to ask your boss for a raise if you've already asked your Prince Charming to write "Cum Dumpster" on your ass.

- EQ

LEARNING HOW TO TALK ABOUT your fantasies can be harder even than acting on them. Expressing your deep or taboo desires to a partner—or even just to yourself—can leave you scared, confused, and feeling extremely vulnerable. But the rewards for doing so can be liberating and life-altering in the best possible way. Sexuality is a part of being human, and there is no single depiction of what is "normal."

Even among people who are used to engaging in other kinky activities, humiliation can be a taboo and difficult subject. It might be easier for you to ask to be tied up or spanked than it is for you to ask to be treated like a piece of trash. That's because even though physical kink is risqué, it has been normalized to a point where people understand both that it happens and the general mechanics of the activities. However, psychological play, and most any kind of embarrassment or humiliation (let alone degradation) can seem incredibly foreign. Even those of us who are into it don't always have the language to describe *why* we're into it or what, exactly, we're into.

> *The topics I want to play with are ableist and body shaming. These are not things I would want to receive around others outside of a specific connection, because I wouldn't want anyone to get the impression that these things are acceptable or inherently enjoyable, or that I seek to diminish the experiences or suffering of others.*
>
> *- albatross*

Nonetheless, communication around humiliation play is critical for both dominants and submissives. Each party's satisfaction and emotional safety depends on it. Yes, negotiation can be a very big communication mountain to climb when it comes to this kind of play, but it is possible! Just like any other kinky topic, it's all about finding the right words and negotiating your needs.

This is the simple, surmountable truth: if you ask for what you want, details and all, you're much more likely to actually *get* what you want. There are many ways to ask for what you want: beg, seduce, suggest, confess, exchange fantasies, write wish lists, use sticky notes if you have to! But if we're aiming at happy, healthy kinksters, making a start in this kind of communication is key. Negotiation is the time to discuss both desires and fears, and it's the foundation of any humiliation experience that leaves all participating parties feeling glad to have had such pervy fun. It's the road to the best time for everyone involved.

> *Before I understood this was a thing that people enjoyed, I was deeply ashamed of my fantasies and thought I was broken. As I matured and learned more, I realized that this is something I can safely enjoy with the right person and not feel like trash afterwards.*
>
> *- Anonymous*

WHAT IS NEGOTIATION?

In everyday use, "negotiation" refers to an informal discussion designed to help two parties reach an agreement. In erotic humiliation, negotiation is specifically about two parties communicating their needs, wants, and limits in order to create and experience a mutually satisfying scene.

I'll share negotiation tips and strategies in this chapter, but it's important to note that there is no one "right" way of negotiating in kink. You and your partner can negotiate orally or in writing; you can create a bare-bones framework or establish every single detail of your scene. No matter how or when negotiation takes place, what's important is that everyone can feel heard and respected, and that you're working toward successful, satisfying experiences.

GENERAL NEGOTIATION TIPS

Before we get deep into negotiation strategies, I want to share four recommendations to keep in mind as you enter any kink-related negotiation.

IDENTIFY YOUR GOALS

If you're in the public BDSM world for any time at all, you'll notice a pattern in the advice you've seen about negotiation, and about the questions negotiations are meant to answer. What do you like? What do I like? What are the activities that we both like? From that, we have a list of activities. Most of these negotiation guides are activity based, but when it comes to humiliation play, there's so much more to it than that.

Maybe you've already covered the basics—"I want to be spanked," or, "I want you to tie me up"—but have you explained what emotional state you are trying to cultivate here? Is the dominant looking to feel a sense of absolute power? Control? A level of sadism? Is the submissive looking to feel controlled? Ashamed? Humiliated? Degraded?

What I'm talking about are emotional goals, or the kernel kinks we talked about in chapter 2. What feelings are you trying to elicit? If you don't understand each other's kernel kinks, then even if you're doing an activity you both like and agree to, you're going to end up pretty disappointed. (Remember my example about putting panties on a man?)

If the word "goal" doesn't feel right to you, you can also think of it as, "Where do you want to be emotionally during and after the scene?" or, "What kind of headspace do you enjoy during play?"

This is definitely one of those things you're better off investing a bit of time talking about first, rather than just trying to work it out through trial and error. Ask specifically, "What feeling do you get when I whip you like a donkey [or insert other activity here]?" Say specifically, "Being whipped like a donkey [or other activity] makes me feel really vulnerable and powerless."

The activity is not the only thing and, in fact, it's not even the most important thing! We all come at the same activity from completely different emotional directions, so the goal here is to be headed in directions that complement one another's desires.

Clarifying these goals saves you time, saves you emotional energy, and gets you to more powerful play. If negotiations are all about activities rather than emotions, a dominant may think that what is needed is punishment, when the sub was actually looking for degradation. Or an activity the dom perceived as dehumanizing may actually feel liberating to the sub. For a dom, understanding the sub's desired headspace is critical to the ability to shape and curate a satisfying experience.

DON'T OVERLOOK TRIGGERS

We talked in the last chapter about triggers and trigger plans. Negotiation is the time to discuss both of those things.

Take the time to find out about each other's known trigger words or actions so you can plan for an experience that won't trip over them.

Here's an example of trigger conversations at their finest:

> For the first Femme Domme video shoot I ever did, I was playing with a female submissive, and before the cameras started rolling, I asked her, "Is there anything I should know?" She said, "You can call me skank, you can call me cum sucker, you can call me streetwalker, but if you call me slut we're going to fucking have a problem, you and me. We're going to have a problem." I answered her, "Thank you for letting me know, because I don't want us to have that problem."

But, as we've discussed, it's not always laid out so clearly. Triggers are one of those little floppy-sided, annoying conundrums: sometimes we don't know about a trigger until we hit it. A person may not remember or know for sure what will trigger a flashback of an abusive memory or negative association. In fact, a trigger could even be hit *during* negotiation if one partner just starts throwing out words or ideas. So, do your best to lay them on the table ahead of time, but then be sure to create a trigger plan, as discussed in the previous chapter, for when things go awry.

DON'T DO ANY NEGOTIATION MID-SCENE

Remember what I said about how being in "sub space" or "top space" can make it difficult to give clear consent? That's exactly why I never recommend negotiating mid-scene. When we're feeling that in-scene "high," it can be very easy to agree to things we'll regret later. When all that negotiation happens before a scene begins, it's much easier to anticipate how particular activities, words, and intensity levels are likely to affect you.

Let me be clear, though, that when I say "no negotiating mid-scene," I specifically mean no negotiating to add *more* to your play—new activities, heightened intensity levels, etc. It is *always* okay for *anybody*, dominant or submissive, to ask the other to turn the volume *down* mid-scene. In fact, I wouldn't even call that negotiation; that's simply communicating about what you need to keep yourself physically and emotionally safe. No matter how carefully you've negotiated a scene in advance, both the submissive and the dominant reserve the right to say no *any time*. This is a necessary part of the trust between the dominant and the submissive. There can be unexpected triggers, and it's important that you're able to escape in whatever way you need to. (As I've mentioned before, what to do if something goes wrong should be part of the negotiation, too.)

CHOOSE YOUR SAFEWORDS

Safewords are a kind of approved language, a verbal **shortcut**, agreed upon ahead of time and used to signal your need to stop an activity or lower the intensity without breaking the scene.

The safewords you use should be easy to remember and ideally won't be in the vein of "No, please stop," since that type of begging and refusal can frequently be an enjoyable, desirable part of the scene. But if "no" is the right safeword for you and all players understand that it *is* being used as a safeword, then by all means go ahead and use it!

Safewords allow everyone to feel more comfortable about engaging in these activities, knowing that if limits are reached, if they change their mind, or if something just isn't fun anymore, they can safely call the scene off. The same can be said about being free to "beg" for the activity to stop, but unless the safeword is used, the scene will not be stopped earlier than desired.

But safewords are just one kind of verbal shortcut—a single word that communicates a full concept. Safewords communicate concepts like "We need to stop now," but you and your partner may want to set up other verbal shortcuts, as well, so you can communicate other potential needs without breaking scene. In terms of pacing or intensity, it's helpful to have a gradient of terms, with meanings ranging from "Please keep going" (a shorthand to respond to check-ins) to "We need to slow down or stop temporarily" to "We have to stop the scene." Many people use a Red-Yellow-Green scale where green means "Go! Go! Go!" and red means "Full stop." But if you're not comfortable with the Red-Yellow-Green system, you can do safewords that fit in with your power dynamic. Something like, "Mercy," or "May I have more please?". Those are ways that you can communicate without breaking the energy of the scene.

But you may have a need for other verbal shortcuts, as well, depending on any physical or emotional wrinkles you might anticipate arising during a scene. For example, I worked with a couple once in which the woman, who was the submissive, had chronic IBS issues, so she would often have to leave the room abruptly mid-scene. When this happened, her dominant partner was always worried he'd crossed a line or triggered her in some way. So, to give her the freedom she needed to book it to the bathroom without worrying her partner, we set up a verbal shortcut. Anytime she needed to run off, she'd shout "There's mutiny!" and he would know exactly what was going on.

These verbal shortcuts can apply to health issues, intensity requests, or anything else you know you might need to communicate about in a scene. (Just keep them short, pithy, and memorable to avoid confusion!)

For more organic communication needs, you can always use strategies like the "stage whispers" I discussed in chapter 4 to ask for what you need without breaking the scene.

Safewords and other shortcuts notwithstanding, it's truly the responsibility of the dominant to know when a scene might be going too far. Due to "sub space," the submissive doesn't always have the consciousness or awareness to use their safeword, so as the dominant, you can't rely on the excuse that they didn't call it so you didn't know something was wrong. As we discussed in the previous chapter, there are subtle ways to check in with your sub (without breaking scene) if you're unsure or would like to double check their emotional state. I understand "top space" can kick in also— the feelings of power and control can at times encourage play to go further than intended. But the dominant needs to remain aware and orchestrate the scene with as much mindfulness as possible.

Submissives, that doesn't mean you're off the hook! Submissives are responsible for being honest about how things are going for them. If you're a sub and you don't want to be disrespectful, then you can first ask for permission to speak and then make a request such as, "Mistress, would you please spread the strikes around more on my thighs?" I *promise* this is not topping from the bottom—but more on that in a minute.

Safety and foundational work can sound like a lot of negotiation and labor, but think of it as an investment. The more you know and the more you prepare, the better these scenes will be. And the more you play together, the better you'll both get at reading each other during a scene. What a great excuse to be pervy more often!

COMMUNICATION TOOLS AND STRATEGIES FOR NEGOTIATION

Negotiation can be done in multiple ways. You can use written lists, forms, journals, decks, etc. to highlight our experiences and interests, or you can sit and discuss things in a private place in a non-kinky capacity. I think it's best to do both if you can, and we'll discuss both approaches in this section.

Whatever approach (or combination of approaches) you take to communicating about your desires and negotiating your encounters, *please* try to let go of your self-judgment and your inner erotic editor. There can be a strong desire to try to explain your humiliation fantasies. If you feel able to do that, fantastic! If you don't, but you still feel compelled to explain yourself, simpler is always better, like: "I'm not quite sure why this turns me on, but as long as boundaries are respected, it doesn't cause me genuine harm, so I just want to go for it." Negotiating and articulating your desires is how you figure out the best way to enjoy your sexuality. It's how you determine where your prejudices came from, whether they were taught to you, and whether they could use a little self-reflection. When you can learn to accept without judgment what turns you on, and what makes you cum the hardest, you get to travel deeper into your own fantasies and explore even further!

It's also important not to judge your partner's fantasies and desires. While they may be activities that don't appeal to you (or that even repulse you), try your best to accept that just because they fantasize about it doesn't mean you have to engage in it. Regardless, they should be free to talk about it. As you let go of your self-judgment and inner erotic editor, let go of your outer erotic editor as well.

BEGINNING ON PAPER

Starting your negotiations in writing may not sound all that sexy, but it's a great way to get your thoughts organized. Writing down your desires, limits, kernel kinks, etc. in private and then bringing that list to your in-person negotiations will mean you have a scaffold to lean on when nervousness kicks in and words fail. You'll be able to be clearer about your fantasies and limits without the endorphin-induced fog of arousal or erotic shame in the way.

By starting with a concrete list, you'll also be able to more easily identify which activities are the highest priority and which ones need to wait until you've been playing for a little while.

If a blank sheet of paper is intimidating, there are a lot of resources you can use to jumpstart the brainstorming process for written negotiations.

Yes, no, maybe lists are a long-time tool of the kink world. You can find generic ones online or check out the humiliation themed option in the *Enough To Make You Blush: Companion Workbook* or my other popular book, *The Yes, No,*

Maybe Workbook, which gives you a ton of space to make notes about the nuances of each interest.

There's another benefit to starting your negotiations in private: You have to *know* what you want before you can ask for it, and spending some time brainstorming alone gives you an opportunity for open communication with yourself as well. Let your mind wander, and let your dirty fantasies out to play. Tell yourself stories or imagine scenes, and see what your response is. If you feel your body start to respond positively, then that's a line of interest you should pursue! If you can't come up with stories to tell yourself, well, that's why they invented the internet. Porn, erotica, and message boards are all excellent places to mine for ideas.

These considerations don't need to wait until you have a partner, either. I strongly recommend that folks work on this solo, even if you're partnered, because getting a sense of your own desires and not your desires in response to someone else's desires can be a more authentic place to start.

NEGOTIATING IN PERSON

The next step (or the first step, if writing isn't your jam) is to schedule time for in-person negotiation before play begins. Remember the bubble we talked about in chapter 2? Where the pressures and judgments of the world don't apply and it's just you and your partner engaging in safe, consensual, mutually satisfying fun? Your in-person negotiations should take place in the same bubble. Whether you're negotiating from within your power dynamic or not (more on that later), negotiations should be a space where each partner can voice their desires, limits, and fantasies with respect and without judgment.

That applies not only to the attitude that you bring to negotiation, but also the environment you create. It's probably not a conversation you want to jump into when you're driving to pick up the kids or when you're both falling asleep.

Here's a pro tip on in-person negotiations: For the clearest communication, make sure that you're both using the same language (i.e., that when you say one thing, your partner hears what you actually mean). Words don't always mean the same things to different people. For example, let's say a submissive requests bondage. They may be thinking of soft silk ribbons and simple, comfortable knots. But if the dominant is thinking of Saran Wrap and duct tape, it's going to make for a very discordant and frustrating scene. Here's an example:

> One of my favorite stories is from one of my first sessions ever as a pro. The submissive had to fill out an online application and check the different activities they were into. This one client clicked "water sports" on his application and then came in for a session. It was my seventh session of the day, so I thought, "Great. I'm going to pee on him and leave him in the tub for ten minutes to soak it up while I take a little break."
>
> So he came in and I threw him in the tub, peed all over him, and left him there while I read a magazine for a few minutes. After a short while I went back into the bathroom and said, "Yeah! How do you like that, little piss slut!?" And he responded, "Isn't water sports enemas?" to which I replied, "Oh, no honey. It's not. You should probably Google an activity before you request it!"

Be specific in the way you communicate, and ask clarifying questions anytime you aren't sure exactly what your partner means. It may seem tedious in the moment, but it will make things much sexier later. (And, let's be real: conjuring highly specific images of what you want to do to each other as you negotiate can be a fantastic kind of foreplay.)

OVERCOMING COMMUNICATION ANXIETY

If you find you can't talk about your desires face-to-face, even after you've done some prewriting, then use a secondary method of communication. Writing back and forth in a journal or sending emails (using a special account if necessary) are great ways to talk to a partner without having to be in the same room. You can even try talking about it on the phone, even if you have to go into two rooms of the same house and call each other's cell phones. Seriously. The absolute, number-one thing is figuring out a way—any way—to make sure you and your partner are communicating clearly and thoroughly about what you both desire.

TAKING THE REJECTION OUT OF "NO"

One of the scariest things about sharing our most taboo and intimate fantasies is the fear that there's going to be a resounding "Eww, no!" on the other side of it.

When we're able to have a conversation and a negotiation, we can agree to be kind in the way we say no (unless it's part of the sexy and enjoyable play to take the "That's gross and I would never" approach, most especially if we're declaring that we would never do those things at the same exact moment that we are, in fact, doing those things).

No does not always mean rejection. "No, thank you," is not the same thing as "Eww, that's gross." One is disinclination and one is unnecessary emotional harm.

When it's approached with curiosity, a no can also be an opening rather than a closing. If you talk about where the no is coming from (for example, "I don't like spankings because you always say you're punishing me for being a bad girl, but I like to be a good girl"), then there's a chance you'll find a more enjoyable version of the proposed activity, or at the very least be able to let go of the sense of personal rejection.

But ultimately, there's no way to take all of the risk out of kinky revelations, which is true about nearly anything. So it's up to you whether or not the possibility of experiencing the kink scenes of your dreams is worth the gamble and uncertainty such vulnerability brings.

CREATING A SCENE AGREEMENT

Some folks like to create contracts to ensure that everyone understands the relationship and is dedicated to the respect of the other person. However, I prefer to call them "scene agreements," because in reality, these kinds of "contracts" would fall apart under even the mildest legal scrutiny, so calling them that can create a false sense of security and commitment.

The scene agreement can include the safewords that will be used, the activities that are on or off the table, the length of the play, a prearranged time frame for renegotiation, and the responsibilities of each partner. Again, this is not legally binding by any means, but it's a way to clearly express your intentions and desires to each other.

NEGOTIATING INSIDE OR OUTSIDE OF THE POWER DYNAMIC

Negotiation can be a great part of foreplay if you and your partner use it as an opportunity to reveal what really gets you going before touching a single toy. And these negotiations can happen either inside or outside of the power dynamic.

For some folks, it's essential to sit down and have a conversation as equals, outside of the power dynamic: "Well, what do you want to do to me?" "I don't know. What do you want me to do to you?" This egalitarian approach can be the only way that some people can feel heard. Speaking directly and without protocol can be an effective way to get at what each of you is looking for out of the relationship or scene.

But I don't think you *have* to negotiate as equals. There are plenty of **truisms** that are pervasive in the kink community, and one I've heard frequently is that negotiations should *always* be egalitarian. I don't think that's any truer than any other truism. It all depends on what works for you and your partner.

The main concern seems to be that if a submissive negotiates from the "lower" side of a power dynamic they will not be respected, but this is nonsense. As long as both partners are being heard, then negotiating within the power dynamic is just as legitimate as any other form of communication. In fact, I personally don't ever negotiate outside of my power dynamics. When I'm talking to the people that I play with, our relationship is established and unwavering. I'm always the dominant, and they're always the submissives. That's how we do things.

For example: wimpy is one of my long-time sub-missives. Our interests match up with a focus on power exchange and his service to me. We understand each other.

But in our relationship, he is not my equal. That is what we have both consented to, and that is the relationship dynamic we have negotiated. He's an equal human being, sure, but in our interactions, he and I are always submissive and dominant, respectively. There is no other way to be. How does this affect our negotiation? Does it mean I don't respect what he has to say when he says it? Well, in the dynamic of our relationship—which we have both consented to—we are not equals, and so we don't negotiate as such. Sure, he's always welcome and encouraged to communicate his opinion and desires, but I'm the final word on everything, because that is *part* of the dynamic. Context is everything here: for us to negotiate outside of this context doesn't even make sense, right? But does he, do I, have a right to back out of this consented-to relationship? Of course. We have negotiated this consent; but as I mentioned before, no matter how carefully play is negotiated, both the dominant and the submissive reserve the right to say no at any point—to a scene or to a long-standing power dynamic.

For instance, wimpy might say;

"Princess, I have an idea for our next humiliation scene, please let me know when you have time and energy for a discussion."

And I would respond with something like;

"Absolutely, my pet! I love hearing your perverted ideas, and I will consider bringing them to life in my own time and with my own flair."

If you've never negotiated from within the power dynamic before, here are a few strategies to get you started:

- Give the submissive an assignment such as writing a list of a dozen activities or words that they find humiliating. (This doesn't have to be thought of as a must-do list; rather, it can be used as a starting point for the dominant to understand exactly what this submissive is attracted to.)

- During a scene, have the submissive communicate the intensity of their experience by asking them to give a numerical rating, which allows the dominant to better orchestrate the physical and emotional sensations.

- Do a "mad scientist" scene where you can be more experimental, loosen up the protocols, and increase the communication methods without worrying about "ruining" the scene.

- Whether you typically have strict protocols or not, you can create a simple ritual that "sets the space" for open communication in the service of negotiation and checking in. It can be anything from environmental elements (like music or a special kneeling pillow for the submissive) to symbolic elements (like the temporary removal of a collar).

TOPPING FROM THE BOTTOM: CAN SUBMISSIVES MAKE REQUESTS?

Being accused of **topping from the bottom** is something that a lot of submissives are very worried about. But guess what? Topping from the bottom doesn't exist. It's a myth I love to bust. "Topping from the bottom" is the idea that somebody in the submissive position is attempting to control what happens in a dynamic or during a scene. A lot of submissives are very worried about that. They don't want to even *seem* like they're exhibiting control. Some dominants are concerned about this as well; they want to make sure that their power dynamic is situated and secure. As a result, concerned submissives hesitate to participate actively in negotiations. (And concerned dominants encourage them to keep quiet.) The subs don't express their desires or make requests from their partners, because they fear that doing so will make it look like they're trying to take control—like they're topping from the bottom.

But here's the thing: If you (the submissive) give me (the dominant) an awesome suggestion and I decide to use it, who's in control? Me! Because *I decided* to use it. You (the submissive) giving me (the dominant) information does not actually usurp any control from me; it simply adds to my ability to exert control. That's really helpful, because it can be hard thinking of all the kinky ideas by myself! For the top or the dominant, it can be exhausting having to think of everything, make it all happen, and keep everyone safe.

But if the submissive is held responsible for helping keep the dominant inspired, they can recognize that they're doing the dominant a service by sharing their fantasies. Of course, the important part is the intention. If you (the submissive) share your fantasies with the expectation that they will happen exactly the way you expect, and if I (the dominant) allow this to happen, the power dynamic *does* get all screwed up. This *is* an attempt to control the scene in a way that has not been negotiated. However, if the submissive states their desires clearly without pressure, simply describing a scenario that turns them on or that they would like to try, the dominant gets to decide what to do with that information. The submissive has placed the power to *execute* on those ideas in the dominant's hands. This fits into the established dynamic and prevents coercive feelings and disappointment.

So, hey, bottoms: don't think about it as topping from the bottom to tell your top what works for you rather than expecting them to read your mind. In fact, it's incredibly important for the submissive to be involved in figuring out how to play. Erotic humiliation is such a personal thing. I always say that the more information I have, the better I'm going to be able to get into your mind to fuck with it. And isn't that what we both want? Yes!

And doms, if you're concerned about losing your sense of control—or if a disobedient submissive is hesitant to share their desires with you—here are a few tips to recontextualize sharing fantasies and helpful information as something very different from topping from the bottom.

One of the analogies I use is that of a brand-new toy. A submissive is like a shiny new toy with lots of buttons and lights, but I don't know right away what all the buttons do. Wouldn't it be nice if my shiny new toy also came with helpful instructions? That's what negotiation is: a set of instructions. I still get to decide which buttons I push and how I will play with my toy, but I need to know that the red button makes you squeal one way and the blue button makes you squeal in a completely different way! I want to push all the buttons!

Dominants that have a submissive that is struggling with this, share this analogy directly. Tell them, "You are a new toy. If you don't come with instructions, how am I going to know how to play with you?" Or say, "You are my plaything, and your will is mine. I require that you expose yourself to me on every level and that you tell me the absolute truth of what arouses and humiliates you so that I may enjoy using you as much as possible." (And if you're a submissive without a dominant, then listen to me, and reread those words one more time.)

These analogies can help both partners understand that information is a gift, not an obligation, and I often tell them that explicitly. I'll say, "This information is a gift, and you giving it to me is going to help me fuck with you in a way that is more fun for both of us. Do you want that? I want that." A submissive is actually doing me a *disservice* if they don't give me enough information; they're making me work harder than I need to.

If, as a dominant, you're still concerned about appearing less controlling simply by asking for ideas, remember that the way you communicate your request for input makes a big difference in how your submissive will respond.

Along with watching your tone of voice, you can switch to detached language, using vocabulary that's very different from your typical communication, in order to make your sub feel intimidated or shamed by the question. Consider the difference between using your most domineering voice to command, "Confess the dirtiest thing that you hope I will never do and yet are really desperate for," and politely (or even worse, insecurely) asking, "What embarrassing thing would you like me to do to you?" In both instances, you're gathering information from your sub as part of a negotiation. However, the way you phrase it makes it either a part of your domination or...not.

Finally, there's one more myth about "topping from the bottom" that I like to bust: The idea that if a submissive "asks for it" then it's not really humiliating is *completely false*. Frequently, the act of asking is humiliating itself, and making a sub list other ways they'd like to play can be a fun part of the scene. After all, submissives have awesomely perverted ideas! The things they share with you will give you a huge clue as to what they're into and what they like.

For example, a long-distance sub disappointed me one time, and I had texted them to tell them I was displeased but had not yet determined what their punishment would be. The sub responded with the perfect idea: "Princess," they asked, "from now on shall I text you only with my nose, while lying flat on the ground?" Amazing. I was thrilled with their idea, and it meant I didn't have to spend my time or energy coming up with one of my own.

The bottom line is this: Don't ever let semantics stop you from gathering information, because information is your greatest tool for fucking with your partner in the best possible way. Stop sleeping on the veritable encyclopedia of ideas your subs are bringing to the table, and instead, start coming up with ways to make them communicate those ideas. Get as much information as you can, and then use it against them in the most deliciously kinky ways! Nobody's going to take away your "DomCard" for that!

10 BASIC NEGOTIATION QUESTIONS

There are many topics that can be discussed during a negotiation, but I've found that the ten questions below cover the most vital information. These questions cover the *how* (protocols for negotiation), the *what* (activities to explore and avoid), and most importantly the *why* (what your goal feeling is for the end of the scene).

1. How are we negotiating?
    In-person/Online
    Oral/Written
    Casual/High Protocol
2. What is the goal feeling (a.k.a. kernel kink) for each of us?
3. What are our soft and hard limits? (toys, words, insecurities)
4. Is sexual contact acceptable? If yes, what kind? What are our safer sex practices?
5. What are the activities we'd like to explore?
6. Are there any health issues (including mental health) to be aware of?
7. What are our safewords? (verbal and nonverbal)
8. Are there any triggers we need to be aware of? (activities, feelings, words)
9. What is our trigger plan?
10. What are the aftercare needs for each person?

BONUS QUESTIONS

Once you've laid the foundation with the ten basic questions above, you can start to dig a little deeper, asking "bonus questions" to learn more about each other's desires and fantasies in order to incorporate those into your play. These can be specifically related to humiliation play, or they can be more general. You'll see a combination of both in the examples below.

- What's the last thing you thought about while masturbating?
- What is your most humiliating fantasy?
- What are three things you would like to explore that you've never tried before?
- Did you have an experience that sparked your interest in and desire for humiliation play?
- What activities do you find humiliating, and can you share *why* you find them humiliating?
- Do you have any fears or anxieties about playing with erotic humiliation?

While talking practically about how to bring your fantasies to life can feel incredibly vulnerable (and often completely unsexy) it's also a critical element of healthy kinky play. Find ways to keep it fun and arousing, or keep it totally separate from your play dynamic—whatever works for you is just fine as long as you and your partner are communicating clearly, thoroughly, and honestly about your desires, limitations, and plans.

WAYS TO PLAY

CHAPTER 6

YOUR MOUTH WAS MADE FOR SOAPING: INCORPORATING VERBAL PLAY

It feels strange to say it, but I love verbal humiliation. It can be playful when she just calls me 'pup' or 'boy,' or it can ramp up with all of the typical terms like slut, cum slut, sissy, and so on. Whether it's mild or more, the words are triggers that take me out of the real world and keep me in hers. Sessions where the verbal humiliation just keeps coming and is elaborated on are incredible. The elaboration might be about what I'm currently doing, something I've done in the past, or something I will be made to do in the future. I think the male imagination

*is a little out of control at the best of times, but during
humiliation play and in a submissive state of mind it can
go crazy. I feel very lucky to have someone that will do
this for me.*

- P

SPEAKING AND VERBAL PLAY ARE some of the most underused elements in the BDSM world. It's a strong statement, but I think it's true.

The act of using words to engage your playmate's brain is so efficient and effective, but people can be scared off because the most effective words—especially in humiliation play—are not words we use very often. Verbal taboos can be one of the most challenging things to get comfortable with, even in more vanilla interactions. Often, it only gets harder when you add any sort of derogatory theme, such as humiliation. You know the saying, "Sticks and stones may break my bones, but words can never hurt me?" Well, turns out, the right words can absolutely hurt too!

So I'm here to say, don't be afraid to use words, even powerful, offensive words. Even the same words over and over if they're the right words. Using words engages the brain, and that's where all the best sex happens anyway. If I'm turning somebody on and teasing them sexually, and then suddenly I simply walk away without saying anything, there's certainly *some* psychological power in that. However, if I look them in the eye and say, "I'm done now, because it's not like you're going to be allowed to cum or anything," how much more powerful is that? Using words to emphasize what you're doing makes all of it even more powerful and memorable.

If you don't know what to say, take the approach of a sports commentator and narrate your perversions or tell them what you're about to do. "I'm now getting ready to pinch your nipples. I'm thinking about it. I like watching your nipples get hard. I'm thinking maybe I might pinch them with my fingers."

Don't forget how tone of voice affects the words you're using. There is a difference between giving an order and making a request. If you sound tentative about calling your submissive names, they just won't have the same oomph—for you or for them. You can even use "non-kinky" vocabulary, but let your voice drip with disdain: "Have you done what I asked?" "Did you do as you were told?" "Are you finished?" This is a really fun thing to practice. We get more comfortable with manipulating language when we use it more frequently. You just have to find your own style.

Naughty language isn't just for dominants, either. If you're a dom, you can give your sub specific words to describe themselves, you, or various body parts. Or you can laugh and taunt as they struggle to create entertaining (and embarrassing) descriptions of themselves. Force them to narrate the action themselves or to answer back in a call-and-response repetition. The power of language goes both ways.

If you're finding that filthy language just feels too, well, filthy, find words that you *do* feel comfortable with (or that you're close to comfortable with). Now practice them when you're in the shower, when you're doing the dishes, when you're driving...anytime you're alone. Try saying out loud, "Cock." "I've locked your cock." "I've locked up your cock in a cage." Or "Cum dumpster." "I am a horny, degenerate cum dumpster."

Try practicing with different tones of voice and getting more comfortable using the words so that, when you're in the midst of sexy time, they flow more naturally from you.

That way you can claim that verbal power and use words to their full advantage when you're playing—ultimately sexier for you and more fun for everyone! If you're still feeling stuck, remember that you are using these terms in a consensual experience, and you're using them on somebody who likes it, so just go for it!

> I had a submissive once who I would tease with a show of bodily contact while he was locked in a chastity device. I would lead him through a demeaning conversation, requiring responses from him, while with one delicate finger, I stroked my body. He was allowed to watch me until I stopped and asked him in teasing tones, "Oh, you're locked in chastity, aren't you? I bet you're just straining to enjoy this. Oh, are you straining? Is it challenging for you?" He was required to answer me, and it was all rather playful and sexy.
>
> Stopping the action and using words to empha-size his restriction, the denial, the submission, and his impotence made a very simple action incredibly powerful. "That's right. I'm in control of your orgasm. You'll look at my body when I com-mand you to look at my body. You will cum when I let you cum."

Using words to emphasize whatever it is that you're doing is super effective. Both new and longtime kinksters tend to think you've got to be a walking thesaurus. I disagree; as I said before, feel free to use the same word over and over, as long as it's the right word. If I'm going to talk dirty, I can work with a comfortable vocabulary of ten to fifteen phrases. Guess what? For many kinksters, repetition is a potent aphrodisiac. It's like eating your favorite meal or listening to your favorite song on repeat. I've been calling my boys "slut" for fifteen years, and it's as effective today as it was when I started, because the enthusiasm, emphasis, and context are still there.

> *I love being called a slut. There's something about that word that I associate with shameful desires, whether it's having too much desire or desiring the wrong things. While I don't mind being called "whore" or "cunt," (which are often used the same way), there's something about "slut" that feels like it's more about me and my desires being wrong.*
>
> *- shameful_slut*

Words also provide a powerful way to explore adventures you might never actually want to act out. By simply describing what you would do, you can create a powerful story that allows you to live out fantasies that might be impractical (or illegal!) in real life.

> For example, I had a couple who was monogamous, but the female submissive was very much turned on by the idea of group sex. So I had her male dominant practice different tones of voice, blindfold her, and then use these different voices while roughing up her body. He also used a variety of sex toys, including a dildo suction-cupped to the wall for her to suck, to enhance her feeling of being overwhelmed by many sensations. Blindfolded, and with the help of her male dominant's voice, she was able to experience being sexually "used" by "multiple men" even though this would have been impossible in their existing relationship.

Also, if physical ability is an issue, imaginative storytelling can be used to access experiences that would be otherwise impossible.

> I had another client who would come to play once every couple of months. He was very into an elaborate good cop/bad cop fantasy. However, he couldn't physically do the actions he fantasized about. So, I would walk him slowly around the dungeon while verbally creating the space for the fantasy by describing in detail what was (hypothetically) happening. "Now I'm going to put you in the trunk of my car and close you up in the dark while I drive for hours. There is no possibility of escape while you are trapped in this tight little space." Fantasies can be impractical for any number of reasons, but with a little creative wordplay, this fellow was helplessly in the hands of a sexually sadistic cop. I seriously loved these sessions and using my storytelling and theatrical nature in fun and powerful ways.

POSSESSIVENESS

The addition of a possessive can completely eroticize and empower derogatory name-calling (*my* cum rag, *Master's* ashtray, you're a cuckie simp for *Me*). A sense of belonging is a natural human desire, and it gets tickled in a very good way when it's attached to derogatory treatment. For a purely platonic example, think of that classic sibling dynamic of "I can beat the shit out of my sister anytime I want, but if anyone else touches her, they're dead."

In humiliation play, the sense of belonging and undercurrent of pride of ownership softens the blow of (consensual) abuse and adds an important layer of connection and intimacy that can "override" the negativity. Being called "that worthless trash" may feel like being dumped in the garbage bin, but being called "*my* worthless trash" could be more like being lovingly placed in the junk drawer or a shelf in the garage.

COMMANDS

Another way to make something humiliating is to make it a clear and unquestionable command.

> For a while, I had a live-in submissive partner who functioned as a domestic servant, doing dishes and laundry and keeping my house sparkling clean. Two years into our relationship, however, I'd stopped making specific commands and started taking my sub's work for granted, assuming they'd do what they were supposed to without my having to ask. Unfortunately, those "assumptive commands" don't tap into the same psychological power of being told explicitly to do something. Eventually, the chores stopped feeling like constructed, sexy activities, and my domestic servant became resentful of the fact that I was being lazy and not helping. So, we changed it up. When they'd get home from work, I'd say something like, "I don't do dishes, so I left them in the sink for my dish bitch. That's you. Get to work." That thirty seconds of effort on my part turned our dynamic from

mundane to magical as my domestic servant bent over backward to please me.

A direct command is one of the lowest-effort, highest-reward things a dom can do, and it's the start of a great humiliation story.

NAME-CALLING AND TEASING

These two are particular favorites of mine. One of my best tips is to use a deck of inexpensive index cards and write a different phrase or dirty name on each card to create flip-through options. You can use technology, like EverNote, but I'm old-fashioned and I really like office supplies! You can also have your partner write different phrases. (Or, if you want it done for you, you can check out my *Filthy Phrases* deck as a great source of name-calling inspiration.) When you're really feeling lazy, you can just say, "Get the deck. You're not even worth the effort to think of dirty things to call you." That in and of itself supports a humiliation mindset, and it lightens the dominant's workload. So efficient!

Another way to use the deck of cards is to hand it to the submissive and say, "Tell me three things you are today." If they pick out "cocksucker," "street whore," and "cum dumpster," that gives you a really good idea of where their desires are taking them. If they pick "cockroach," "inchworm in the mud," and "mold in your toilet," that gives you a good clue in another direction. It frees the submissive from having to verbalize their particular desires, and it provides the dominant with insight and a start to the humiliation play. This turns both parties into something of a mutual inspiration society.

BEGGING

The act of begging is one of the most fundamental (and fun!) ways to use verbal play. Hearing someone beg for an activity, either something they really do want or something they're hesitating about, will tap into the psychology of humiliation. For the submissive, the acknowledgement that they want something dirty or taboo (begging for an orgasm, begging to be led on a leash) is a way to allow the power of their own desires to be used "against them." And for the dominant, making someone beg for an activity they "don't want" (within the consensual and negotiated list of activities of course!) is a powerful way to fuck with their head. Listen to the submissive struggle to adjust their tone of voice to convince the dominant that they really desire whatever they're being made to beg for.

> One scene I had was with a male submissive who wasn't really into pain but was willing to suffer a bit for my amusement. I had a great little hand-held electrical zapper, so I sat elegantly on the couch, held it dangerously close to his delicate erection, and had him beg me to shock his cock with it. The first few rounds sounded very unconvincing, so I continued to give him little zaps on his cock, and after each one he'd have to say, "Princess, *please* shock my cock again," as sincerely as he possibly could. We worked on tone of voice until he sounded as desperate for it as I wanted him to sound. If he didn't request it genuinely enough, then I shocked his cock. And if he did request it genuinely enough, I also shocked his cock. By the end, the humiliation of having to beg for it did put

him in the right mindset, so eventually he really was begging for the electric zap in a way he never thought he would. It was a real win-win for me and a real "Ow, ahhh!" for him.

If, as the dom, you would rather wait to see the "final" version of begging, you can also have the submissive practice while looking in a mirror. Making them look themselves in the face while practicing "being pathetic" is super humiliating, and again, it lightens the dominant's workload!

QUIZZES

I love to quiz my submissives just because it's fun. It evokes a classroom feeling of pressure and constant evaluation. Think of the punishment potential for wrong answers!

"What's my favorite color?"

"I don't know."

"You're useless!" *Smack, smack, smack!*

A dominant can quiz their sub on academic questions (state capitals or past presidents), which they might actually know, or stick to more personal topics (birthdays, favorites, and experiences) where you're more in control of whether they have the right answer.

FORCED SELF-HUMBLING

The amusement that can come from watching a submissive try to articulate words while they're turned on is rather enjoyable. Make them think of dirty things to call themselves, and watch as they struggle to bring forth appropriate terms from their muddled and aroused brain.

Start with something like, "I'm going to humiliate you by calling you names." Then, move into, "I'm not even going to bother to think about calling you names. Get me the deck!" Then, "I'm not even going to bother to read the deck. Humiliate yourself while I listen and laugh at you."

PRAISE KINK

Remember when we talked about praise kink earlier in the book? Well, now it's time to shine! (Or, rather, to force someone else to shine.) It can be so embarrassing in all the best ways to "force" someone to stand (or kneel) in front of you and receive (or give themselves) compliment after compliment after compliment. So many people have been taught to defer and deflect flattery and praise that being required to endure it creates a sort of embarrassment trap of kindness. Personally, I like to make them maintain eye contact with me while I deliver one of my renowned "aggressive pep talks," where I shower the recipient with unrelenting compliments and an insistence that they have what it takes to reach their goals/grow as a person/sparkle and shine bright. It's embarrassment in the service of self-esteem!

CONFESSIONS

One of my favorite ways to get to know somebody is to ask, "What did you think about the last time you jerked off?" Typically, people will give you the most palatable version of whatever they were most recently thinking about, but here's my best tip for getting actual confessions from people: Ask them no less than three times. So after the first response, ask again: "Now, what's the *actual* dirtiest thing that you thought about?" They might respond, "Well, okay, I was thinking about this kinda dirty thing." Then you go in for the kill. "Okay, but what's the filthiest, dirtiest thing that you've thought about recently to jerk off to?" That's when you get the good stuff! People tend not to just spill the beans right from the get-go. Occasionally you'll get someone very blunt or uninhibited who will share their deepest desires right away, and that's great. But if they don't, being persistent and really digging in will lead to a confession that is much more useful for you. Three times, with increasing pressure and seduction. Try it!

Confession is a huge psychological setup. Having someone talk about a memorable experience and forcing them to describe and relive the experience is a way to get their brain going while they share information. They've got to process it and figure out a way to articulate it, and they have to cope while admitting to, blushing about, and confronting their own desires.

MANTRAS

I had a submissive that did my laundry for many, many years. Once, he screwed up something with my socks pretty badly. Luckily, this boy had a foot fetish, and so forever after, when he'd put my dirty laundry in the washing machine, he'd have to pick up each stinky sock, sniff it, and say out loud, "I'm a stinky sock sniffer."

He'd have to do this at the laundromat, and it became a mantra for him. He'd come in the door and I'd say, "What are you?" He'd say "I'm a stinky sock sniffer."

I like alliteration a lot, and it makes a mantra memorable. Use your imagination. Come up with a catchy rhyme! "Daddy's boy is Daddy's toy." Make it something that stays with them.

WEARING SIGNS

Verbal play can be written down instead of spoken aloud, as well. For example, you can create signs for the submissive to wear around their neck, either temporary ones that won't last long or more permanent signs that are laminated. I used to buy those plastic office bathroom signs at Staples, drill two holes in them, and add chains to turn them into waterproof, wearable placards for my watersports enthusiast subs. I had another sub who was particularly into sissification and would wear self-made laminated signs saying things like "sissy bitch cocksucker."

Wearing a sign, or having a submissive wear one, hearkens back to *The Scarlet Letter*, or to dunce caps in old schoolhouses. It takes an internal, "shameful truth" and makes it public and inescapable. It's the verbal equivalent of being locked in the stocks, and even if nobody else sees it, the externalization of that "truth" can be quite powerful.

Words have an incredible amount of power, and we can use their overarching social context along with our own recontextualization to create psychological arousal.

MORE WAYS TO PLAY

- Both players focus on one or two words, and play with tone of voice to imply different meanings.

- After each smack with an impact implement, the dominant makes the submissive say a specific phrase.

- When out in public, the dominant can whisper into their sub's ear what they plan on doing to them later.

- While forcefully stimulating the submissive, the dom requires a confession of a humiliating fantasy.

- The dominant creates a ritualized phrase the sub must use while begging to have an orgasm.

- The sub is commanded to come up with ten dirty, descriptive words for themself.

- Together, the dom and sub create a "thesaurus" of words that turn them both on, to be used in scene.

- The dom instructs the sub to rewrite songs or nursery rhymes using dirty words.

- Using washable (or permanent!) markers, the dom writes naughty words all over their sub's body.

CHAPTER 7

THIS LITTLE PIGGY WENT TO MARKET, THIS LITTLE PIGGY SUCKED TOES: FOOT FETISH

I've enjoyed some teasing "forced" sock sniffing while being masturbated, having/getting to worship her feet while she read a magazine, playing "chase the feet" at a dungeon party and another time on a lawn.

- MULTIPERV

FOOT FETISH IS ITS OWN huge umbrella, beneath which there are a wide variety of kinks, including humiliation play. It's important to note here that there are a lot of foot fetishists who do *not* consider humiliation to be an element of their experience at all. For many years I hosted private FootNight™ foot fetish parties in Boston and Baltimore, as well as attending many others throughout the United States, so I've spoken with a *lot* of men and women who enjoy this fetish. Statistically (and anecdotally), I'd say more men have a foot fetish than women, but for a majority of the women I met modeling at foot parties (as well as in my general kink event experience), once they were introduced to the joys of foot fetish, their enthusiasm became authentic.

In recent years it seems that the idea of the "foot fetish" has had its cultural moment. These days, the idea that someone could be "into feet" is practically blasè. However, although there is a cultural knowledge that something broadly described as the "foot fetish" exists, there is very little general understanding of what these fetishes really are—of what it is about feet that actually gets people off. Personally, I've found there to be an infinite number of ways foot lovers can get extremely detailed about the specifics of their desires. From the color of nail polish to the shape and length of a toe to the intensity of a foot's scent, there is a wide range of interests under the idea of "foot fetish."

Foot fetishes open up plenty of opportunities for public play as certain activities, such as receiving a foot rub, won't arouse any suspicions that something sexual is happening (as long as you're each discreet about your appreciation for the experience!). But like anything, adding a public element can hugely up the ante in terms of both humiliation and risk. Go ahead: have the submissive kiss your feet upon public dismissal, or put them in a rain puddle and use them as a stepping stone to protect your feet (and give them the added bonus of being walked over). But be careful not to attract unwanted attention or offend those who didn't consent to be part of your scene. I recommend you read Chapter 19, which is dedicated to public play, before venturing outside.

For those who do enjoy an element of humiliation with their foot fetish, the focus is frequently on feelings around being "low" and "on the level of feet" (both physically and culturally), or being embarrassed about having a foot fetish at all. A foot fetish is another great one to "use against them" with verbal play, focusing on how much feet turn on the submissive.

Certainly there are many foot lovers who have fastidious tastes and like the feet they're worshiping to be completely clean and scent-free. However, when humiliation is involved, strong foot scent is often a big element, and for some, the smellier the better.

Foot scent is an extremely personal aroma, and while there are things you can do to accentuate the smell of your feet, it's pretty hard to change their odor outright. Some people just don't have very smelly feet (which, in this case, might be disappointing!), so if that's the case, you have to find "enhancements" that work for you. I recommend wearing leather shoes or very old, used athletic shoes. I've also found that fur-lined suede boots can be very effective at upping the stink ante if worn barefoot or with stockings/socks.

The term "foot worship" covers a few different activities. Passionate kissing, licking, and sniffing are naturally worshipful ways for a submissive to express their love for feet. You can imagine a logical conclusion here, and how humiliating it can be (or can be made to feel) for your submissive to cum by rubbing themself against your feet.

Foot accessories also tend to be a separate but overlapping interest. A submissive's foot fetish might be focused on bare feet, or it might require the addition of socks, stockings, or shoes and boots. Each of these can be used to customize the humiliation and add to the vocabulary available for the verbal aspect. Having the submissive "polish" boots with their tongue is popular, and there are some who engage in "bootblacking" play from a humiliating perspective. This submissive might put together a care kit and commit to being responsible for the tender care of all the dominant's boots.

"Dirty feet" is another subset of foot fetish, and as usual, people desire this to varying degrees. The extreme version might include walking around barefoot in a parking lot until the soles of your feet are black with asphalt, then making the submissive lick them clean. Of course this isn't sanitary, so you both take on a much higher risk, as the dominant could step on something and be injured and/or the submissive could become ill from licking up actual dirt and god knows what else from the pavement.

As I said, not everyone with a foot fetish is there for the humiliation. But for those whose fetishes overlap between humiliation and feet, there are many ways to incorporate the two, using elements described in some of the other chapters.

MORE WAYS TO PLAY

- The dom makes their submissive kneel inside a closet with their face smooshed into used sneakers.

- The dom tickles the sub's feet. With a bit of bondage, this can be a fun way to make them lose physical control.

- The sub licks their meals off their dom's feet.

- Before allowing the submissive to eat, the dominant crushes their food under their boots or rubs their dirty feet in it.

- The submissive acts as a footstool, or as a rug for the dominant to wipe their feet.

- After wearing a pair of socks for a few days, the dominant encourages the submissive to breathe deeply through the foul-smelling cotton.

- The dominant uses their feet to put light (or rough, if desired) pressure on the sub's genitals.

- The dominant commands the sub to get low to the ground to crawl behind their feet/heels/boots.

CHAPTER 8

I THINK YOUR LAMPSHADE IS CRYING: OBJECTIFICATION AND DEHUMANIZATION

Most recently, my Master and I have begun to explore pet play and we have found that dehumanization is particularly humiliating to me, such as being made to eat out of a bowl on the floor, walked around on a leash while crawling on all fours, performing tricks (such as rolling over), and being potty trained.

- ASHLEY ROSE

DEHUMANIZATION IS GREAT FOR THOSE who are overly cerebral or tend to think themselves into a frenzy. It's a very zen kink practice where the sub has one single focus: to exist as a particular item or creature. Personally, I classify animal play as mid-level, because the "animal" can still express personality through interaction. But when someone becomes a lamp or table, that's as basic as it gets. "Hold this light still. Balance this plate on your back. Stay curled up as a footstool." These demands create a feeling of tunnel vision that can be a mental relief from the daily, nonstop demands of decision-making and processing. Dehumanization frees the sub from all that pesky upper-level mental function.

One of the most simple dehumanization techniques is using a hood (with or without eye and mouth holes) to cover the whole face. For longtime partners, this can be an easy way to make the submissive less recognizable, making it easier for the dominant to act with more emotional distance, if that's the energy you're going for.

Differently abled bodies will need to work around these suggestions to find what's best for them as kneeling like a footstool or having the face covered, for example, may be infeasible. There's an adaptation for almost everything. To find it, you just have to consider the kernel kink and the goal you're trying to achieve with the activity. Dehumanization is more about tapping into the spirit of the animal or object you're becoming. So if you want to do puppy play and you're in a wheelchair, your movements can still have a sense of scampering if you express that feeling in a way that is within your ability.

Like with any physical activity, you should take into account your *actual* abilities. I love pushing boundaries, including physical limits, but safely and within reason. If you have bad knees, don't curl up for an hour straight without stretching out. You may not be able to move afterward, or you might pull a muscle that prevents you from playing further or, even worse, intrudes on your everyday life. The fantasy of being bound in rope for six straight hours to keep you in that table position might be the hottest jerk-off fodder ever, but there's a translation that has to happen for your human body to endure it in real time.

BECOMING AN ANIMAL

One type of dehumanization is animal play. Not everybody who engages in animal play finds it humiliating. There are plenty of people who love puppy, kitty, or pony play who find it liberating—they are finally free to be that puppy, kitty, or pony that, as adults, they've "outgrown." But many people also find it dehumanizing to be turned into something less than our glorious blessing and curse of humanity. (This goes back to the kernel kink and the need for doms to know their submissives in order to create a scene that satisfies everybody.)

Puppy play sessions were some of my favorites when I was doing professional work, because it was a low-impact way to play with embarrassment and humiliation. I dealt with a lot of cis-het male guys, and I would say "I'm going to turn you into my dog. Are you ready?" I would get very into character, and though they might initially be trepidatious, they would eventually get very excited.

I'd start by saying, "Okay puppy, okay puppy! Who's a happy puppy?" Then, when my sub responded in human English, I would say, "Uh oh... puppies don't talk. No, puppies don't talk. Puppies bark! Let's hear the puppy bark. Does the puppy bark?" And I'd give him that expectant look one gives a dog who has received a command until he offered a half-hearted little bark. Then, I'd use the voice that let him know he's a bad puppy because he was not listening, and I'd say, "No, I only play with enthusiastic puppies. Let's hear enthusiasm." That would make him try harder to please me.

"Ruff, ruff, ruff!" he'd bark, and he'd earn a little reward.

"Oh, you know enthusiastic puppies get to sniff my crotch! Do you want to be a good, enthusiastic puppy?" All of a sudden, he was the best dog on Earth.

"Ruff! Ruff! Woof woof woof!" Now he had the idea.

"That's right," I'd praise. "Good puppies get to sniff my ass." He'd bark more, he'd sit up and beg, he'd do tricks. Then I'd pull out a flopping dildo (make sure it's not a low-quality jelly dildo) and play fetch the bone. "Oh, you want the bone? You want the bone? You want to fetch the bone?" He would be humiliated by this ridiculous toy, maybe emasculated by it. He'd be dehumanized by my tone, by my repeated and simple commands. He'd bark anyway. "You do? You want to fetch the bone? You want to fetch the bone?" He was dehumanized because I had stripped him of language, but just because he couldn't speak doesn't mean he couldn't beg for it.

"Ruff, ruff, ruff!"

"Fetch the bone!" I'd throw the wiggling thing across the room and he'd go scrambling over to pick it up. "Only with your mouth!" I'd scold, reminding him I'd dehumanized him by taking his opposable thumbs.

"Ruff, ruff, ruff," he would bark around a mouthful of wiggling dildo. Just a simple puppy.

Perfect.

Here's one of my favorite mind fucks for puppy play: Get the same size can of beef stew as dog food and swap out the labels, but make them smell the actual dog food before dumping the beef stew in the bowl. The look of horror on their face is priceless. It is amazing, as they can't help but balk while you're standing there saying, "Good dogs eat all that food, so you better believe *you're* going to eat that dog food!"

A less intensive way to use food in puppy play is to use Coco Puffs (which look like dog food) and, if you can find them, Kellogg's Scooby Doo-themed cookies in the shape of dog bones.

OTHER ANIMAL IDEAS

Kitten Play: Use strings and ball toys, rope bondage, scratching post punishment, spray bottle training, litter box training, tongue bathing the master, neck biting as in cat sex, curling up in someone's lap, or purring.

Pony Play: Many people don't find pony play particularly humiliating, so more of a work horse/donkey approach may be needed. This could include transporting items with saddlebags, whipping, bridle/harness walks, or "facilitated breeding procedures."

Barnyard Animals: Play "Old McDonald Had a Farm" using masks from the costume shop, and have them make the appropriate sounds.

MORE WAYS TO PLAY

- The sub and dom explore different types of collars and leashes together.

- The dominant purchases an extra large plastic neck cone and, after putting it on the submissive, instructs them to complete a domestic or sexual task.

- The dominant teaches the submissive to do tricks such as lie down, sit, roll over, or beg.

- After shopping for a dog cage with the dominant, the submissive spends time inside, working on "crate training."

- The submissive eats all meals out of a special dog bowl.

- The dominant makes the submissive hump their leg, a pillow, or a stuffed dog.

- The submissive is forced to eat a peanut butter treat off the dom's genitals.

- The dominant demands sexual positions suited to a dog.

- The dominant gives the submissive a puppy bath and grooming session.

- Rather than in the toilet, the submissive is forced to pee on a puppy pad.

- The submissive wears a "cock leash" or a leash with clamps so they can be led by their genitals.

- The submissive sleeps on a large cushion at the foot of the dom's bed.

BECOMING AN OBJECT

One step further than animal play along the continuum of dehumanization is turning people into furniture. This is also called "forniphilia," a term originally coined by the famous pornographer Jeff Gord.

> I had one client who struggled with overthinking, who had a very hard time just...stopping. So, we went to Walmart to shop for a lampshade. Now for the most part, people are too self-centered to care what you do in public, as long as you're not obscene or overtly sexual (more on that in the Public Humiliation chapter). However, if anybody asks, you should come up with a quick story to explain your errand. So when we went shopping, I had my submissive stand there as I tried lampshades on him, one after another. As we were doing this, a woman walked by and gave me a puzzled look, to which I smiled and simply said, "He lost a bet." She smiled back and went on about her day.

> When we were back at my dungeon space, I put the lampshade on and handcuffed his hands to his dick. I'd attached a tape-wrapped cord to the

light bulb so he could hold it, illuminated, next to his genitals. Now, this is dangerous, people. If he drops the bulb, then there's broken glass every-where. If he hits himself with the hot bulb, he'll get burned. You want to be hyper-aware of these risks, but sometimes the element of danger is part of the attraction. Proceed with caution. (Remember R.A.C.K.)

This submissive had to reach a still place in his mind in order to keep the bulb from touching his skin. He could think of nothing but being a lamp, and suddenly, this person who didn't know how to stop had found his zen. It was a miracle. The practice of dehumanization is actually a freedom for a lot of people.

Being human is really complicated. Being a lamp is not.

And if either partner finds it too boring or low engage-ment to simply act as furniture, you can up the ante by add-ing in a predicament or focus element. For example, if a dominant is having trouble getting their footstool to stay at the height they want (though the submissive might be try-ing!), give them something to focus on. Get a tape measure and tape the end to the submissive's chest. They then have to watch that tape measure to be sure they're staying at the desired height until the dominant desires something else.

OTHER OBJECT IDEAS

Art: Turning people into art and making them stand and pose in different ways can be great fun as well. You can do this during a private scene or, for the kinkily advanced, take your art to a party! That's a good time, people. That is a very good time for all.

Coat Rack: With a bit of creative bondage, anyone can be used as a coat rack, held in position with hooks or hangers attached. And of course you can use a cock ring on penis-having individuals for an extra peg (a hat hook, perhaps) with the threat of punishment should the "hook" fail.

Ashtray: For the smoking fetishist, being made to hold or eat the ash from a cigarette or cigar can be the perfect kind of objectification.

MORE WAYS TO PLAY

- While eating a food that produces a lot of waste (for example, an orange or seeds or nuts), the dominant turns the submissive into a trashcan by chucking the waste (the orange peel, the peanut shells) at them.

- The dom turns the sub into a table so the sub has to balance items such as a drink or magazines on their back or other body parts

- The sub acts as a footstool for dom. (If knees are an issue, try having the sub curl up in the fetal position instead of kneeling.)

- During appetizers, the sub acts as a platter for charcuterie, sushi, or other finger foods. (Bonus points if this happens at a party.)

- The sub acts as a canvas for fingerpaint or splatter paint designs.

BECOMING AN IT

The furthest down on the dehumanization ladder is turning someone into an "it." This is where they are stripped of all identity and all usefulness, becoming even less than an inanimate object. Being treated as a piece of property—a lamp or a footstool—takes away the stresses of humanity but leaves some semblance of usefulness. Being an "it," on the other hand, strips away even that small bit of purpose. It's incredibly dehumanizing in the best kind of way.

Ignoring or not acknowledging a submissive is another way of dehumanizing them. Talking about the sub with other people while the sub is there, putting their nose to the wall and going on about your business, and being disinterested while they masturbate are all ways to make the submissive feel insignificant. (Do make sure that abandonment isn't a trigger before this kind of play.)

WORTHLESSNESS AND INFERIORITY

An effective (and potentially seriously triggering) way to explore dehumanization is to attack someone's value or worth. This can be done in a variety of ways, but it is best done with someone who generally has high self-confidence (but enjoys being knocked down a peg or twelve). Verbal emphasis on being "less than" (less than either the dominant or someone specific, or less than everyone in general), being rejected, and being insignificant can feel brutally dehumanizing.

A personal favorite way to invoke a sense of worthlessness and disposability is to turn your submissive into trash by stuffing them into a trash can! (This will, of course, depend on body size and ability.) Bonus points for throwing more trash in after them. Even making someone stand in a trash can while you throw leftover food at them is powerful and sexy in that degrading sort of way.

OTHER IT IDEAS

There are no other It ideas. That's the point. When you're an It, that's all you are, and there's nothing you can do.

CHAPTER 9

COITUS HUMILATUS: SEX AND MASTURBATION

my Sir likes to make me squirt at play parties, in front of people! I'm told "it's such a turn on" and it "makes Him feel proud" but I'm so embarrassed by the mess and how much i actually enjoy the embarrassment factor.

- ANONYMOUS

MUCH OF KINKY PLAY DOESN'T involve traditional sexual interaction, but that doesn't mean that it can't. The use of humiliation during intercourse taps into strong psychological experiences while incorporating more "traditional" erotic play.

In fact, combining traditional sex acts with humiliation is one of the most popular ways to explore erotic embarrassment play. During an interview on his Masocast podcast, host Axe used the phrase **erotic slut shaming**, which was so accurate that I've adopted it into my philosophy. Erotic slut shaming centralizes the erotic body and arousal as the target of torment, and it is anecdotally the most commonly desired type of humiliation play (statistically, too: nearly 80 percent of respondents to my 2014/2015 survey chose the word "slut" as their favorite dirty talk) . In fact, this kind of play is so omnipresent in the kink world that one of the most common comments I get after I teach a humiliation class is, "Oh my god, I didn't even realize I was already doing that!"

One of the reasons this play is so popular is that the expectations, limitations, and beliefs about what is "acceptable" sexual behavior provide a deep pool for us to play in. If society didn't tell us it's "bad" to be sexual, then we wouldn't have such a powerful response to expressing our sexuality. By reveling in the "obscene" acts of perversion, we experience a deep sense of social rebellion that can be downright intoxicating.

DIRTY TALK DURING SEX

As we've discussed in the previous chapter, this can be used during any of your humiliation play sessions, but when used during intercourse, verbal humiliation tends to focus on the taboos surrounding arousal and sexual interaction.

When we play with consensual nonconsent dynamics in erotic slut shaming, being "forced" to perform sexual acts can release the "responsibility" of sexual desire and response. This is exactly why verbal commands are so popular, whether a primal growl to "strip naked, now," or a mocking demand to "lick and suck each one of my toes *slowly,* and show me how horny my feet make you."

This can create a special sort of sub space that I like to call "slut space," which has strong elements of submission but is mostly about the performance of increasingly insatiable sexual cravings.

THE ORNAMENTAL FUCK DOLL

Oh, to be a mindless body whose only purpose is for their holes to be used for the pleasure of others, or to have access to a horny servant happy to service you at your whim—this is the desired state for so, *so* many kinksters. We live in a society that cherishes thinking and the mind (well, theoretically at least), so to be made into nothing more than a decorative sex toy is demeaning in the most delicious way.

If your submissive has a high sex drive and an exhibitionistic streak (even if that streak has to be strongly, um, *encouraged* if not required), then keeping them horny, available, and aesthetically pleasing to you while simultaneously stressing that their own worth defined by their sexual service to you can be a magical formula for erotic embarrassment that can increase in intensity depending on how shy or liberated they feel.

For an especially shy submissive who shrinks from the limelight, use items that are beautiful and eye-catching, such as a butt plug with bling or nipple clamps with rhinestones and bells, to make them feel ostentatious. When I'm feeling particularly generous, I also love to turn out all of the lights, instruct my submissive to pleasure themselves, and then use a flashlight to make them feel like the obviously exposed focal point in a slightly unnerving (and yet liberating) way.

PLAYING THE WHORE

Sex work continues to be rather taboo in society, though (as a former sex worker) I'm thankful there are more mainstream conversations happening that are breaking through the stigma. The concept of sexually "selling your body" as a prostitute, stripper, or other sex worker is frowned upon and treated as if it's inherently dehumanizing, and this is where the Pervert Paradox comes into play. We can know that sex work is real work and that real sex workers deserve respect and to be treated with dignity, but we can still choose to play with and explore the very real stigma around it within consensual erotic adventures.

Ironically, for actual sex workers, the experience of being paid is more empowering than not. It's seen as a sign of respect. But indoctrinated whorephobia equates being paid for sex acts with the lowest of the low. So for some kinksters, the mere act of being paid (or paying for) sex acts is enough to spark a sense of erotic humiliation, and for others, the low-value or low cost of real or imagined sexual services is where the most potent degradation lies.

For example, one of my submissive's favorite fantasy-to-reality desires is to be rented out for "forced bi" blowjobs, and I frequently remind him that his skills are so unimpressive that he wouldn't even be able to get five dollars a pop but would have to settle for three.

KINK SHAMING

Even though I'm *very* proud of being a kinky (a.k.a. sexually creative) person and I've dedicated my life to destigmatizing some of the most misunderstood kinks, there's a lot of fun to be had with the "eww, you're such a pervert" approach.

I recently had a kinky play request that hit all the right notes for me, including kink shaming as the core theme. I roleplayed as a young woman who had never been exposed to anything kinky before and had just discovered my "letterman's jacket" boyfriend had a foot fetish. I was of course shocked, disgusted, and demeaning about this "weird, perverted sex thing" and mocked him while "forcing" him to tell me about his depraved fetish fantasies and stuffing my feet into his face.

"I didn't know this kind of freaky stuff turns you on, what a sex wierdo! You're seriously telling me that rubbing my stinky feet all over your face makes you horny?! I can't wait to tell the whole cheerleading squad!"

"FORCED" BISEXUALITY

"Forced" bisexuality uses the dynamic of consensual non-consent. This usually involves "forcing" a heterosexual man to have sex with another man, but it can be applied to anyone. At one kinky camp event I attended, I was asked to participate in a forced bisexuality scene with a woman who had never had any experience with same-gendered sexuality and had always felt nervous. She wanted to be "forced" so that she could get over her fears and finally see how it would actually feel. What started out as a humiliation scene wound up becoming very empowering for her.

Forced bi play is an excellent time to use the "ramp up, don't dive in" ethos. There are many ways to play before you ever actually involve another person. If I have a submissive man who's interested in forced bi play, then I like to warm them up through a series of sessions that introduce him to increasing levels of realness. I start with having them use their own fingers or mine to demonstrate technique, then I graduate them to a non-phallic dildo or a blow-up doll, then to a more realistic dildo with balls. And after multiple sessions with the theme of, "Isn't it going to be fun when it's a flesh cock in your mouth? Can't you just imagine it?" *then* we'd bring a stud-cock in for a scene.

TEASE AND DENIAL

I've said it before, and I'll say it again: The best part of sex takes place between your ears, and that's particularly true when kink is involved. Bodily contact can be fleeting, intense, and physically exhausting. Mental contact and the whole process of sex, however, can last as long as you want, be as intense as you can imagine, and energize rather than drain. A great way to engage the mind is through the art of teasing and denial. At their foundation, these activities are based on arousal, anticipation, and control. There are a lot of crossover feelings and actions in chastity play (covered more in-depth in the next chapter), because chastity play allows for a lot of teasing, leading directly into denial.

A great way to cause arousal in a sub who is chaste (by command or with a locking chastity device) is to strip or dance erotically for them. I've worked as a stripper, and I've taught stripping to many other women. Invariably, people feel self-conscious or even silly taking on this role, but the truth you need to remember is that your partner is turned on by your body and your confident use of it. (Knowing that your sexy dancing produces literal torture should help with the confidence part.) I consider my stripping experience my

ProDomme boot camp, because after learning to control a room full of drunk men, one or two submissives is a breeze! I discovered my dominant self through stripping because I love the tease and denial aspect of it. It's so powerful for me, and it can be humiliating for those watching who feel intensely impotent, vulnerable, and judged for their arousal.

Whether you're stripping, dancing, or teasing in any other way, make yourself the object of lust and worship but not of contact. Wear stockings and heels, and make your submissive follow your feet on a leash as close as they can without touching your feet. Every time they hit your feet they get cropped, and if they do it perfectly they get to worship your heels. Or do the same with boots and a belt buckle. Find out what body part or bit of paraphernalia turns your submissive on the most, and turn it against them, then show no mercy. You hear me? No mercy!

There are also more intense forms of denial than simple teasing. If your submissive is more turned on/humiliated by orgasm denial, try masturbation within a rigid framework. I love to do "masturbation minutes," and a kitchen timer is one of my favorite kinky toys. You can totally Pavlov the submissive into being turned on by just the sound of ticking. (One of my submissives can't go to Thanksgiving dinner with his family, because every time he hears a timer "Ding!" he gets an immediate hard-on because, for four years, he wasn't allowed to masturbate unless I had a kitchen timer going. You'll learn why in a minute.)

You can also require a stroke count, or use veto power to make them stop no matter how close they are (this is called **edging**, but more on that a bit later). Teasing and denial lead to sexual frustration and the torture of being close—close enough to see the promised land but denied by the will of a powerful dominant.

"FORCED" ORGASM

The opposite of orgasm denial is the forced orgasm. The "forced" in forced orgasm is pretty tongue in cheek of course (because orgasms are awesome and feel nice, so how can they be forced?), but there are ways to make an overload of pleasure go from "Oh, yes, that feels so good.." to "Oh fuck, please make it stop."

Prostate milking is the use of therapeutic (and in our case, relentless) prostate massage to induce a forced orgasm. This is done by inserting an (ideally gloved) lubricated finger into the submissive's ass and pushing on the front wall of the rectum in a persistent motion until an orgasm is achieved, which may be followed by a less pleasant, more unusual sensation (all bodies are different though, so your experience may vary).

Cock milking and cunt juicing (a term I just invented) take a similar persistent approach of overstimulation as a path to orgasm and, in some cases, orgam after orgasm after orgasm. It can be very effective for turning pleasure into pain and for turning a moaning submissive into a begging, twisting, pleading pile of mush. Using your hands is incredibly intimate (and possibly exhausting) so you can also improvise some bondage to keep a vibrator, butt plug, or other sex toy in place.

If you really enjoy turning your partner into a fuck doll (or are self-transforming into the enthusiastic sex slut of your dreams) you can also invest in a sex machine. It's a particularly helpful device for the insatiable orgasm seeker and can free up the participating dominant to focus on verbal humiliation or other forms of play. Sex machines are also a disability assistive device! Depending on how seriously you take your kink and sex play, it can be a worthwhile expenditure.

SPEAKING OF MASTURBATION...

Masturbation is by necessity an incredibly personal activity, and many people have internalized a lot of shame about it, making it an ideal playground for humiliation.

First, learn the masturbation habits of your submissive. Getting them to discuss this is often its own form of humiliation. Then, once you understand their default preferences, fuck with those preferences. I have a strong absurdity kink where I really like to laugh as often as possible, and forcing someone to jerk off in a way other than their default, in a way that's not nearly so efficient, creates hilarious predicament challenges. Personally, I enjoy the confusion and struggle of watching someone try to cum left-handed much more than the bondage predicaments that most people imagine.

Assign the submissive to masturbate in a position other than the one they normally use; if they usually jerk off lying down in bed, make them stand up—watching someone masturbate standing up when they normally don't is fucking awesome! Their knees buckle, they struggle to stay upright, and it becomes a battle against floppy muscles. As you start to see these clues that they're close, you can begin to deny orgasm. You can say, "Your knees are getting a little wobbly. Let's give you a moment to recover, and then we'll let you get back to where you were." I also love to heckle them: "Knees straight! Knees straight!" Controlling your sub's masturbation and pleasure this way, you might require them to masturbate for a certain period of time without climax in order to make them feel displayed and frustrated.

You could also choose a position or method that you know makes it hard for them to cum, with bonus points if it makes them feel self-conscious to have you watching them struggle. Have them hump a pillow or use their nondominant hand. If they normally masturbate with sex toys, deny them sex toys because that might make it harder for them to cum, or vice versa. Mix things up, too. Throw a wrench into it to screw up the idea of cumming. "I'm just going to wrap your dick in bondage tape, and you're totally welcome to jerk it off. You can cum...if you can. Go ahead and try."

A great way to humiliate someone is to have them masturbate while you ignore them. For example, I might have them stand in a corner while I attend to my email, or file my nails...you know, more important stuff. They'll eventually say, "Princess, may I please cum?" and I'll say, *No.* Are you kidding me? Keep jerking off!" or "Wait!" and then, "Okay, you can keep doing what you were doing." It can also be more related to my distraction: "You're going to jerk off and be denied as long as it takes me to write this email." From my experience, this is also a great way to incorporate getting shit done! I've got quite a lot to accomplish in this life. I don't have time to be perverted all day, but I try to fit it in.

(Caution: This strategy is likely to bring up more non-erotic feelings than you would expect. Lots of people have abandonment issues, making it one of the more frequent obstacles to this kind of play. If someone has abandonment issues and the idea of ignoring them didn't come up when you were negotiating, it could go really wrong. Have conversations about triggers and emotional needs before trying anything new.)

Masturbation schedules are another one of my favorite ways to play. I used to do this a lot with long-distance submissives, because it allowed for a lot of control without much physical access. I would set specific masturbation appointment times, telling the submissive they could cum Tuesday at 9:00 a.m., Friday at 3:35 p.m., and Saturday at 11:15 p.m. If they missed those times, they were shit out of luck. The effort that they went to to make sure they were home or in a private place at the appointed times was astonishing. That's a purely mental experience of domination. There's no physical exertion of any kind for me. It's literally just me saying, "I am controlling your orgasm by allowing you to cum at these specific times or not at all." Another, less structured option is to randomly set timers on their phone so that when the ringer goes off, they have ten minutes to find a place to masturbate or they lose the chance. Or text them a code word randomly with the same restriction. You get the idea. Whether pre-organized or spontaneous, it's a great way to play with orgasm control.

I might also specify how often they were allowed to masturbate. Sometimes I would just say, "You have three for the week. Use them up as you want." I had one long-term submissive who was definitely an excessive masturbator, and he would just bust all three out and then spend the entire week begging me for more. I just told him, "No. No. No. No. Still no." All week long, my philosophy was, "I gave you three. You should've spaced them out."

EDGING

If you have closer proximity and more time, a very subtle form of torture can be found in edging. Edging is a pattern of masturbating right up until you're ready to cum and then stopping and letting the build-up die away. It's a classic masturbation game. It requires a lot of control from both partners, but it's intense and intimate and can result in exquisite agony or explosive orgasm. You get to pick.

My favorite form of this game is what I call "Masturbation Minutes," and it uses an old-fashioned kitchen timer as a sensory spark. I turn the dial and set it to three minutes and then instruct my submissive to begin pleasuring themselves. They are not allowed to reach the peak, and as the dial tick, tick, ticks right in front of their nose, they must keep themselves on the edge. Then, when the timer goes off—"Ding!"—they must keep their hands raised for another three minutes while I whisper torturous words or simply smirk as their hips sway in desire. Then—"Ding!"—it's time for your hands to go to work again, and we do this over and over until they're practically weeping for release.

MORE WAYS TO PLAY

- The oral worshipper uses a "cocksucker mirror" or a traditional mirror to watch themselves giving enthusiastic oral sex.

- The submissive is made to beg for sexual acts, the more depraved the better.

- The dom uses bondage to keep the submissive still while a vibrator is used for repeated and extended orgasms.

- The submissive wears a remote controlled vibrator or a butt plug when out and about. (Be discreet, though, and don't get yourself into trouble!)

- The dom gives a male submissive an obvious hard-on at a local kink party and doesn't let them hide it. (Making a submissive wear a strap-on under their pants can be equally effective.)

- The sub is required to watch "extreme" porn that they're embarrassed to be turned on by.

- The sub is "forced" to use sex toys that are too large or uncomfortable.

- The dominant "catches" their submissive masturbating.

- The dominant fucks their submissive with their fett or with a strap-on attached to their boots.

- The sub is instructed to "seduce" a blow-up doll until they orgasm with it.

- The players make a sex tape together (revealing or concealing theiridentities) and post it on an amateur porn site.

CHAPTER 10

LEARNING TO LOVE THE LOCK: CHASTITY AND ORGASM CONTROL

*When tied and helpless or in chastity, I love
being reminded, either verbally or through action,
that I am powerless. The humiliation comes in teasing
about the power situation, not in humiliating me
as a human being, which turns me off.*

- A

Your orgasm is such an intimate and individualized thing. That makes it all the more fun to fuck with! To have control over someone's orgasm or to give up control of your orgasm is incredibly powerful.

Acknowledge the lust, embrace the lust, celebrate the lust, emphasize the lust...and then deny its consummation. When you emphasize the denial, it becomes this great erotic cycle: You get really turned on, and then you're denied, which turns you on, and then you're denied again. We love sexy cycles.

I think chastity play is my top way of humbling and molding a man. Unlike the other activities, it doesn't stop when the session is over. It's unrelenting, 24/7, cruel and very, very real.

- Lanie

We talked a lot about orgasm control in the previous chapter—especially the section on masturbation—but with this kind of play, the emphasis is not just on control, but on restriction and more intense denial.

WHAT IS CHASTITY PLAY?

Chastity can be about submission, pain, teasing and denial, or even about bondage. It's often used as a way to keep one partner focused on the sexual pleasure of the other partner. In short, it's a pretty versatile way to play.

Chastity is the control of orgasm, but even more specifically, it's the *denial* of orgasm. Now, obviously, being chaste means not having sex, and in this case not cumming, either. But it's not just about denial. As you saw in the last chapter, forced orgasms are their own art, and they can even be incorporated into the denial. Sometimes orgasm control is just denial, sometimes it's a shorter period of denial and then force, and sometimes it's just force. Who doesn't like to choose from such a perverted buffet?

So, let's talk about the denial and control of orgasm using either devices or mental control. Of the two, mental control is the most important, because here is the biggest key concept of chastity play: You can't depend on the device.

If you don't remember anything else about chastity play, remember this: You can fetishize the device, and you can use the device as a tool in many different ways, but if the submissive who is locked up does not have some kind of mental/emotional commitment to the chastity, no device will stop them from achieving self-pleasure.

Spontaneous or unconscious (or nocturnal) orgasms can still happen in devices and without intentional stimulation! It might simply be the friction from the device, or a psychological state of arousal so strong that no physical touch is needed. For example, my submissive wimpy, who's been locked up for years, would commonly have an orgasm (without ejaculation) when we would go shopping (which is a very good use of orgasm, in my opinion). I knew a foot fetishist who could have a hands-off climax simply by looking at my soft soles from across the room. These accidents can happen no matter how mentally committed your sub is, device or no device! They're more common for penis owners, but they're possible for anyone. When they do happen, you can just make them part of the play by doling out "punishments."

All that is a long way to say that devices don't actually prevent orgasm, and if you rely solely on any of them, you will be sorely disappointed! It does not matter what kind of locked device you have; if your sub wants to defeat it, they can. Orgasm always finds a way!

I had one submissive who came to me and said, "I'm a habitual masturbator, but I'd like to start doing some chastity play." I had done some other training with him off and on before, but he had some commitment issues in the past, so I said, "All right, we'll give it a shot, but I'm going to give you a test first. You'll come see me Friday night. I'll lock you up myself, and you will stay that way until Sunday afternoon, when you will come back and I will release you. Then, if you pass the test, we'll discuss further training." He agreed, so when Friday night came, I locked him up and said, "I want you to send me a text message tomorrow afternoon to let me know how it's going, along with a photo of the locked cock cage. I'll see you Sunday afternoon." Saturday afternoon I got a text:

"I'm sorry Princess."

I responded, "What are you sorry about?"

"I let myself out."

"Well, how did you do that?"

"......Bolt cutters."

This is why most devices aren't dependable. He had just spent hundreds of dollars on this device (he was not a wealthy man), he had spent weeks begging me to lock him up in it, and he knew he had one shot. Still, he nearly cut off his weiner with a pair of bolt cutters to get the fuck out of that cock cage. See? The pervert-MacGyvers of the world can get through pretty much anything. And particularly if you have a clit, getting around chastity is ridiculously easy. You just grind on your own device!

DEVICES MAY NOT BE DEPENDABLE, BUT THEY SURE ARE FUN

That being said, if wearing a device is a big part of your desired play and you want it to genuinely contribute to effective control, consider investing in a custom chastity device that will give you safety and security.

Chastity cages can be made from plastic, silicone, and steel. Another less known option for short-term play, created by The Stockroom, is called the Penis Prison. It's a pouch made of leather or rubber that fully encases the genitals and locks them away snugly. Quality can vary wildly between producers and types of devices, so it's worth doing research and buying from reputable manufacturers (see the back of the book for a list of resources). Fit matters, especially for long-term use, because chafing can get very uncomfortable very quickly.

There are some interesting combinations of chastity and tech being explored, but beware: As with any smart device, there's a risk of being hacked, giving a stranger control of the device or getting it stuck permanently. It may be a sexy fantasy, but it can be a scary reality (and it's already happened—just Google it).

Chastity belts are also an option, but their focus is on preventing penetration, and they typically aren't designed for long-term use. Orgasm is still possible, just no direct contact or insertion. The basic chastity belt design hasn't changed much since the sixteenth and seventeenth centuries, though, in addition to leather, now you can purchase them in modern materials such as stainless steel or heavy vinyl, or with a snap-in butt plug.

SUCCESSFUL SEXUAL DEPRIVATION

When it comes to chastity play, like any other kind of kink, if you want to be successful, you and your partner have to negotiate your goals together. Figure out how to commit to each other and to what you're trying to do before you even think about discussing devices. Talk through your goals for chastity play—whether you're looking for control, sexual focus, or something else—and have the submissive create a short statement of intent outlining why they want to remain chaste. This can serve as an affirmation for the submissive to come back to when they're horny and struggling with the commitment, and it can also outline ways for the submissive to channel their urges into something that furthers the play and serves or pleases the keyholder. (For example, if a submissive is feeling horny, they may channel that into massaging the keyholder's feet, maintaining their commitment while catering to their dominant.)

At this stage, mental obedience—and not devices or any other logistical bells and whistles—should be your primary focus, as it is a crucial, crucial aspect of chastity play.

If your sub has a serious commitment and an earnest desire to use a device to keep that comment, however, the whole process can be fun. Picking out a device and locking into it can be really sexy and powerfully symbolic. It's a great reminder of who's in control—an industrial-strength authority your sub can rub up against—but it won't do the work of keeping your sub chaste or keeping their orgasm under wraps.

So that's the thing. The buck stops with the person locked up. You could do as little as put a rubber band or large piece of tape on their genitals as a "device." It's really about that mental reminder, as opposed to the dependency on the lock. The best lock is in your brain.

If you do use a device, keep these safety tips in mind:

- Many chastity devices use plastic locks that feature a serial number to avoid a cheat who snips the lock off for a quick wank and replaces it with another. These are very efficient, simple, and safer in many cases than a full metal lock.

- Cheap plastic devices are known to break and snap, so strenuous movement while wearing them can create a sharply dangerous situation near your most sensitive bits.

- If your sub is long-distance or has to spend a long period of time wearing the device, consider the need for hygiene. If you're containing a very damp, intimate area, things can get unhealthy very quickly. If I've got somebody locked up for a while, I want to make sure their genitals don't get infected and turn green in the name of preventing another orgasm. (Okay, probably a slight exaggeration, but you get the idea!)

- If you want to avoid the submissive having a pleasurable time on wash day, only allow them to use a vegetable scrubber or something on the harsher spectrum of personal hygiene items, like a rough loofah.

- If you use a metal chastity lock, having a second key is a necessary safeguard, and it can be incorporated into play as well. Have your sub's key held by a friend—bonus points if it's *their* (kink-friendly) friend (it can be incredibly humiliating and emasculating to tell a friend that your dick has been locked up and you're not allowed to cum unless someone else says you can). You can freeze the key in an ice cube (that's by far the most popular, but make sure they know *not* to put it in the microwave in an emergency), or you can hide it somewhere and then put the instructions for finding it in an envelope. There's no end to the possibilities!

Orgasm is one of the best things we have to look forward to. It is our basest, simplest pleasure. Glory in the power of taking that from someone, or in willingly giving it up. It's chicken soup for the sadistic soul.

HOW CAN CHASTITY BE USED?

Now it's time to think outside of the box (or cage, as it were), to explore all the different physical and psychological ways you can use chastity in your play.

LONG-TERM/SHORT-TERM

For a lot of players, the goal is to use a device for an extended period of time, from multiple days to multiple weeks or months. But if the denial impetus is powerful enough, even hours can be exciting.

CHASTITY AS GENITAL BONDAGE

You can also focus on the physical sensation restriction chastity devices provide (including the short-term Gates of Hell for folks with a penis) and add them as a bondage element. Layered with other types of bondage, such as leather or spandex sleep sacks, rope, or metal cuffs, a device can increase the reality of total restriction.

For flexible kinksters with a scrotum and penis, the Scrotum Pillory (also known as The Humbler) is great for short scenes where a mixture of humiliation, physical discomfort, and gential restriction is the desired goal.

TEASING AND DENIAL

Once a sub is locked down, think of ways to put them in the path of arousing stimuli. Send them to a BDSM event or to a strip club, or even do a dance to entice them yourself. If they're into feet, have them sit in a park and watch the flip flops or boots walk by. Use the device to really heighten their discomfort, emphasizing control of their sexual experience starting with the most basic building blocks of their arousal.

EARNING ORGASMS

Chastity is a great tool for domestic training while keeping the focus on the dominant's pleasure (see below). You can set up a gold star system, where the submissive can earn orgasm privileges by finishing chores or giving the dominant orgasms. Example rule: For every three dominant orgasms the submissive earns one.

A ROLL OF THE DICE

Sometimes it can be helpful to use an outside authority to determine how long the submissive is locked in chastity. Get a set of dice (you can even use *Dungeons & Dragons* dice with up to twenty sides!), then roll them to determine the number of hours, days, or weeks the submissive is forced to stay locked up!

SEXUAL FULFILLMENT FOR THE DOMINANT

Of course, just because your submissive is being denied doesn't mean you have to be! There are plenty of other ways they can take care of your sexual needs, from giving blow jobs and hand jobs to using a gag with a dildo on it.

USE YOUR WORDS

There's a strong verbal element that can be used in chastity play. I like to emphasize the denial when I talk to a chaste sub. "I know what you want to do, but you can't. Because you're my locked-up little whore, aren't you?"

RUINED ORGASMS

This is where the dominant actually lets the submissive get to the point of cumming and then does something to ruin it. There are two types of **ruined orgasms**: active and passive. A *passive* ruined orgasm is when you allow the submissive to get to the brink of cumming and then remove all stimulation and let them hump and thrust uselessly. An *active* ruined orgasm is when you allow them to get right to the brink of cumming and then inflict some sort of distraction, frequently involving pain or impact play. My orgasm-ruining technique is a little nontraditional, but it works! When my subs are getting close to orgasm, I require them to request permission.

When they ask, "Princess Kali, may I please cum," I tell them to go ahead, but then when they're right on the verge, I jump at them and yell in their faces like a deranged haunted house ghost. It's silly and startling and one of the less classy kinky things I do. But, while it's not a terribly thought-pro-voking technique, it is effective! Of course, punching them in the balls or cunt-punching are also options, if you know what you're doing. I'm an equal opportunity crotch-puncher.

Another verbal trick for ruining orgasms is describing things that are totally not erotic. I've heard people aim at non-erotic distraction by saying things like, "Your grandma's titties in your face." Even I'm a little perturbed by that, and I've been known to say some pretty extreme things, but to each their own. I once heard a story of someone who intentionally whis-pered an awful boss's name in her partner's ear. Use what you know. It's important to find something that works and doesn't bother you to say either repeatedly or loudly enough to throw their mind off the orgasm track. Really annoying sounds also work. You could use an air horn or klaxon as a classier version of my good old-fashioned jump scare.

You can also use physical distraction: Suddenly putting a plastic bag full of ice against their genitals when they're about to cum tends to work pretty well.

Another approach for ruined orgasm is what I like to call "Mangled Masturbation," which is when you disrupt their usual masturbation patterns and favorite forms of self-plea-sure with a position or sensation that makes orgasm much more difficult to achieve. For example, the submissive who usually masturbates lying down is required to stand and keep their knees straight. Or if they prefer standing up, have them lie on their back with their feet in the air (this is a great position for humiliating masturbation scenes regardless, by the way). I've even given my submissives a cardboard tube or piece of sandpaper and then commanded them to use it to attempt to cum.

ADVANCED CHASTITY PLAY

Many of the suggestions I've already made in this chapter could be considered extreme by some players. Yet there are ways to raise the intensity even higher for those who are looking for a more severe experience.

KALI'S TEETH

Particularly for short-term play, add an extra element of discomfort with a device called **Kali's Teeth** (not my actual teeth, but a device that has spikes on it and can be worn alone or with a chastity device). It can be excellent as punishment or for a masochistic submissive.

PRINCE ALBERT AND CLITORAL HOOD PIERCING

If genital escapability is an issue (a cock and balls can be quite the little houdini) and/or the submissive is deeply committed to staying locked and is willing to go the extra mile, you can also introduce a Prince Albert piercing, which is a metal ring pierced through the urethral opening of the penis and coming out of the undersurface of the skin at the tip of the penis.

This allows for both additional locking (I once commanded a submissive to be pierced in this way so we could lock the chastity device directly to his piercing) and with increased sensitivity, which can be quite an erotically torturous scenerio.

A clitoral hood piercing can be used in much the same way (though typically it can be more awkward to connect it to a chastity belt) but rather than increasing the denial, it is more likely to increase the sexual stimulation.

OTHER WAYS TO PLAY

- For long distance play, the dom requires photo proof at regular intervals of the securely locked device.

- The sub creates an affirmation of commitment, including a specific distraction for when temptation strikes—something non-erotic or, better yet, pleasurable for the dominant.

- The submissive is required to do a sufficient amount of enthusiastic begging before being allowed an orgasm.

- The dominant sets a goal for their submissive to have as many orgasms as possible in one day, night, or weekend and rewards them if they reach the goal.

- Combining chastity with financial domination, the dominant assigns a fee amount for key-holding, orgasm allowances, or both.

- Using exact (or flexible) days and times, the dominant schedules orgasms for the submissive. This can even include specific instructions for specific days, such as "hands-only Thursdays," "anal toy Saturdays," etc.

- For disobedience or masturbatory slips, the dominant and submissive predetermine punishments. Anything from an extended chastity period to unofficial aversion therapy in the form of repeated painful forced masturbation.

CHAPTER 11

YOU'RE DOING IT WRONG: GENDER FUCKING AND GENDER FAILURE

GENDER, LIKE SO MANY SOCIAL norms, is a construct that we are all "performing" in one way or another, whether we identify with the gender we were assigned at birth or not. If you're presenting feminine, are you feminine enough? Are you *too* feminine to be taken seriously? Same if you're presenting masculine—are you "manly enough"? Are you so ripped and toned that you can't possibly be anything other than a dumb jock? Everything from clothing preferences to body form to speaking style is critiqued as being right or wrong.

My good friend Sinclair Sexsmith says it this way:

We have unattainable standards of gender, most people will fail at gender at some point in their lives, and just about everybody has a wound or insecurity about that. And so it's prickly, you know? It's a vulnerability because gender in and of itself is an impossible standard to meet, right? Gender is an unattainable standard, and we're not *supposed* to reach it. We're supposed to strive for it and fail and then feel bad and keep working harder, right? That's kind of how the system is set up. And so when someone is saying you fail at gender, it's humiliating and vulnerable, because we feel that way sometimes, but it's also a relief to feel someone tell that truth. Oh, that's hot. So it's like, "You're right I am failing."

- Sinclair Sexsmith

In other words, we have unattainable gender standards in our society, no matter where anyone is on the spectrum, and *everyone* fails to meet those standards. It's as if we're all Goldilocks in the three bears' house, and "just right" doesn't exist.

But here's the good news: Because there is so much (ridiculous, unfounded) judgment tied up in gender performance, gender provides a variety of rich opportunities for erotic humiliation fun. In general, there are three ways we can humiliate each other based on our inevitable failure to perform gender "correctly."

1. PLAYING WITH CONTRADICTORY GENDER

One of the most common ways to play with gender is "sissification"—making a male-identifying or male-presenting person dress and behave like a woman. Sissification is so common, in fact, that the next chapter is dedicated specifically to that kind of play, but it's not the only way to play with contradictory genders.

I'd estimate that 90 percent of contradictory gender play is about increasing feminization, because—at least according to cultural norms—isn't it just so embarrassing to be a woman? So you'll see men asked to dress as maids and do domestic service (you don't often see women ask to do this because it's already seen as women's work), or you might see a dom "force" a butch lesbian sub to adopt a femme style and attitude. But you don't often see women being "butched up" as a form of humiliation, because men and "masculine" traits are actually higher up the power ladder.

Still, making an extremely femme person wear male clothing or embody masculine or stereotypically male behaviors might be *personally* very humiliating, even if our culture doesn't see it that way. Consider how it might feel for a woman who loves to wear designer dresses, put on full makeup, and style her hair meticulously—who finds power in being ultrafeminine—to be asked to throw on overalls and leave the house in a baseball cap and no makeup. Done consensually, there's a lot of potential there for some fun, binary gender-based erotic humiliation.

2. GENDER INADEQUACY

Gender inadequacy play—based on the idea that, whatever gender we're playing, we aren't doing it well enough—tends to go both ways a little more freely than contradictory gender play.

For women, female-presenting, and nonbinary people, this capitalizes on the idea that someone isn't performing femininity to the appropriate degree. For a popular example, think about *Miss Congeniality*, where the comedy (for viewers and supporting characters alike) centers tomboyish FBI agent Gracie's utter discomfort in the hyperfeminine beauty pageant world. She feels totally ridiculous being put into these tight dresses and having everything from her eyebrows to her butthole waxed, and while the people around her see it as a transformation into a "real" woman, she sees it as demeaning and humiliating.

> *It was the moment after an impact scene at a local play party where I had a much-needed cry during the session. My Master at the time looked at me and pointed out how my makeup was smeared, then proceeded to make it worse by saying I looked like a filthy whore. I then had to stay that way for the rest of the party until we went home. It was amazing and horribly humiliating, as I was raised to always be presentable.*
>
> *- TeasingFire*

Since our culture tells us that femininity is less-than (even as it tells us to be more feminine), the performance of femininity is often perceived as humiliating regardless of who's performing it. That's why gender inadequacy play works so well for non-femme-presenting women.

BETA MALE EMASCULATION

With men, playing with gender inadequacy often takes the form of beta male emasculation. One of the most common interests expressed by the cis men who responded to my survey is being emasuclated as a "beta male," particularly through sexual denial (including cuckolding) and being mocked for a lack of sexual prowess. This is deeply related to expectations of masculinity and the idea that alpha males—of superior physical strength and masculinity—are the only ones who are worthy of "getting laid."

So, in playing with the "beta male" idea, a dom may humiliate a male submissive by telling them they're "not a real man" and so they're a loser, or that other men are far more masculine, attractive, and worth fucking.

Where does the beta male kink come from? In my experience, and based on the anecdotes that came up over and over again in my erotic humiliation survey, the preference for this kind of play often—though certainly not always—takes root when a guy gets cheated on. He then deals with that feeling of inadequacy over not being able to satisfy a woman by eroticising the humiliation. He flips the script, turning perceived inadequacy into an avenue for sexual pleasure.

This isn't necessarily the same as sissification or forced feminization because, rather than dolling a man up like a woman and really playing that feminine angle, what the dom is saying is that the sub is so bad at being a man that he might as well be disqualified. That said, beta maleness can absolutely be a step on the path toward sissification—after all, if you're playing "not man enough," then why not take it even further and start leaning into femininity?

*I understand how women get offended when guys
say they want to be crossdressed and humiliated
for that. And some of them probably do truly think
of women as inferior and of being made to look
or act like one as an insult. I think there are many
others, though, that see or fantasize it as not a
"woman=bad" thing but as more of a "man fail"
thing, along the lines of "well, you're clearly not any
sort of man, maybe we should dress and have you
act as more of a girl, yes, you're clearly more suited
to that. Sort of telling a giraffe he is not a good
giraffe but makes a great raccoon. The racoon isn't
bad or lower but it certainly doesn't have the same
characteristics of a giraffe and reinforces that he
doesn't have enough natural characteristics to be
recognizable as the species he claims to be.*

- multiperv

CUCKOLDING

Cuckolding is another way to play with gender inadequacy
in humiliation, and it seems to be a timeless interest as it's
often discussed online and there are more than twenty thousand books related to the search term on Amazon. (Clearly
there's a market for it!) While this type of play is commonly
presented as a heterosexual dynamic, kinksters of any gender or sexual orientation can enjoy it and can adapt the language to suit personal needs. Cuckqueaning is the gender
opposite of cuckolding, with a male dominant enjoying sexual activities outside of the relationship while keeping the
submissive woman celibate entirely or having her service his
and his lovers' needs.

Cuckolding and cuckqueaning are generally based the dominants' pleasure and right to take another lover, often because of the gender sexual inadequacies (real or fantasy) of the submissive. As always, when playing with cuckolding and cuckqueaning, remember to make sure you're on the same page in terms of motivation and goals. Humiliating someone for their "sexual inadequacies" can be a huge turn-on, but it can also go horribly wrong; there should be careful negotiation before this kind of play.

Traditionally, the male submissive is the cuckold—he's not considered "man enough" to please his partner, so he has to watch while his partner finds satisfaction with "real men"— but anyone can play this way depending on the focus of the activity. It can involve other partners if you're polyamorous or have an open relationship, and you can even incorporate cuckold fantasies into your play without bringing other people into your real-life relationship.

For example, you could have a strap-on the submissive has to suck and "prepare" for sex. Or the submissive could give the dominant a lengthy oral sex session while the dominant describes in lurid detail what they'll be doing with their "real lover." Add a bit of public play by sending your male submissive to the store to buy Magnum condoms.

It is important to note that, particularly with cuckolding, race play has a tendency to sneak in in an undiscussed and potentially problematic way. Race play isn't always off-limits; it just needs to be negotiated carefully in advance and desired by all parties. There are lots of people who enjoy extreme taboos like race play; it's just important to find them intentionally instead of just expecting people to engage with your personal kink when you launch into it willy nilly. This is true with any kind of play, of course, but it can be especially easy in cuck play to get "swept away in the moment" and incorporate racial issues spontaneously, which is dangerous. This is because some kinds of cuck play, fetishized primarily by white men (and sometimes white women), reference desires like, "I only want you to fuck Black men," or "I only fuck Black men." Even if language like that is not explicitly included, or even consciously considered, a lot of cuckolding desires are rooted in racist beliefs about Black men being overly sexual, sexually ravenous, well-endowed, etc., which leads to the racist connotation that a white man whose wife fucks a Black man is more humiliated than if the same woman had fucked a white man. Of course, cuck play isn't always racist, but because those elements can sneak in, especially among white players, and it's important to be particularly aware of avoiding nonconsensual race play in these scenarios.

3. OVERPERFORMANCE OF GENDER: BIMBO AND HIMBO-IFICATION

Remember how I said that gender performance, by its very nature, is something we can't win? Here's proof: I just talked about all the ways we can humiliate each other for not being "good enough" at gender presentation, but guess what? Being "too good" is *also* grounds for humiliation, because it takes away your credibility.

When a woman or female-presenting person is the object of this humiliation, she's considered a "bimbo"—too feminine to be good for anything other than sex, and certainly too feminine to be smart. Think Elle Woods, from *Legally Blonde*: She's an incredibly intelligent, powerful woman, but because she was raised to focus on her looks—and because she authentically enjoys dressing and behaving in very feminine styles—she is constantly written off as nothing more than a real-life Barbie doll treated like she should be embarrassed.

And it happens to men, too: when a man or male-presenting person is hypermasculine, with enormous muscles and a perfect jawline, even if he's actually a thoughtful, philosophical bookworm, he's assumed to be a dumb jock—all brawn and no brains.

In real life, these assumptions are damaging and demeaning at best. In the world of erotic humiliation, however, they can lead to some seriously satisfying play.

MORE WAYS TO PLAY

· In a "forced exercise" scene, a dom either mocks a masculine-identified submissive for inadequate strength or reduces them to nothing more than their muscles.

· On a trip to a thrift store, solo or as a couple, the dom chooses an outfit that accentuates or contradicts the submissive's usual gender performance to build a scene around.

· During a sexual encounter, the dominant focuses the verbal humiliation on how, even though the submissive is "unfuckable" and "undesirable," they're settling for fucking them anyway.

· In a bully roleplay scene, the dominant focuses on the gender failures (too girly or masculine, or not girly or masculine enough) of the submissive.

· The submissive becomes a "dolly," with the dominant treating them like arm candy and saying demeaning things to others about their intelligence all night.

- Using "praise kink," the dom has the submissive show off their gender in the spotlight (either literally or figuratively) and catcalls them in gender-affirming ways until they're squirming in embarrassment.

CHAPTER 12

HE WAS A LITTLE GIRL WHO HAD A LITTLE CURL: SISSIFICATION AND FORCED FEMINIZATION

My semi dressing in public has intensified.
Last month we went away for a weekend trip,
and my instructions were to pack only female clothes.
I also was shaved nude completely with my nails and
toes polished. We took in a dance, an apple festival,
and a winery that weekend with me [cross]dressed.

- LEXI ALLEN

SISSIFICATION AND "FORCED" FEMINIZATION ARE often conflated, and both are stereotypical associations with humiliation play. These may seem like the same thing as cross-dressing, but that's just one activity that can be an overlapping inter-est with sissification. In other words, sissification is always cross-dressing, but cross-dressing isn't always sissification. How can you tell the difference? Typically, sissification focuses on extremely feminine, ruffled clothes and is often deeply submissive with a strong dose of humiliation. Forced femi-nization is another term to describe the activity of turning a man into a caricature of a woman, usually with an attitude of consensual non-consent. Cross-dressing, on the other hand, might use a variety of clothing styles and may or may not incorporate a submissive or humiliating viewpoint.

I've found that, especially with this kind of play, it's most important to make sure your goals and philosophies line up. My first experiences with sissification were with cis-het men saying, "Turn me into a woman so I feel humiliated." That atti-tude is deeply rooted in misogyny; most men are brought up thinking that being called a "sissy" or a girl is the worst possible insult. I, on the other hand, think being a woman is glorious and beautiful and graceful, and for these men, act-ing like one of us for a few hours should feel like the ultimate honor instead of the ultimate degradation.

So when men would come in and say, "Turn me into a woman to humiliate me," that really frustrated me until I understood that what many of them were saying was, "Objectify me, because I'm socialized to think that only women are objectified." What they wanted was to be treated like sexual objects. This is where I learned catcalling is not *only* power-based (although a lot of it is) but in the pure and consequence-free theater of the mind, it is often intended as a compliment. In these submissive men's minds, the thought of being objectified sounds awesome. To have somebody look at them and say, "Mmm, yeah, I'd totally tap that," is thrilling. That objectification (when I removed the hateful mocking of women implied by some kinds of sissification) was something I could provide.

So I took those clients and said, "I'm not going to turn you into a woman, but I'm going to make you strip for me, and I'm going to throw pennies at you." This way, they started to learn the feeling of objectification without having to associate it with femininity. This was one of my early lessons in the importance of figuring out the desired feeling (the kernel kink) before attempting to indulge someone's request. Remember the importance of aligning your mutual goals with your philosophies. With this kind of play, for example, they got the feeling of being objectified without me having to compromise my feminist philosophy.

Gendered fabrics are one of the most absurd aspects of modern society, so satin and lace are useful fabrics because of their femininity and the sensual physical sensation of wearing them. Panties are one of the easiest and most popular sissification tools. Frills add the right touch to almost any garment. One way to add a public element is to go shopping together at a lingerie store. When I do this as a female dominant with a male submissive, I pick out a bunch of panties for myself, and then I hold the panties up to him and say quietly, "Do you think your little pecker will fit in here? Mmm, I don't know." Then the sales lady will walk past, and I'll say, "Do you think these will fit him, or do you think we need something a little stretchier?"

It's not an obscene question, and we're not trying to sexualize others or involve them in our play without their consent (don't be creepy or give kinksters a bad name!). But places like Victoria's Secret or Frederick's of Hollywood are great. They've met people at various junctures of the gender expression and kink spectrums; you will probably not be their first. It's entirely likely that they will smile and say, "Oh, I don't know. Why don't we try some of these?" and a public humiliation scene will just take off. No need to get explicit with it—even discreet breaking of gender norms can be powerfully effective. You might see sales associates or other customers whispering over in the corner, or maybe they won't care at all. Either way it's okay. As long as you're buying something (and not being overtly sexual or engaging them in your play without their consent), they don't care who it's for.

MORE WAYS TO PLAY WITH PANTIES

- The submissive picks out, wears, and presents themselves to the dominant in a pair of panties.
- A bra and stockings really complete the look; the sub picks them out.
- The dominant "catches" their partner wearing panties or masturbating into panties.
- The submissive wears panties under regular clothing.
- The dominant creates a "panty schedule" for the submissive, with certain rules for each day of the week (e.g., wear red on Fridays or satin on Sundays).

With sissification, you need to make sure that you've negotiated well and discovered what works and what doesn't. There are plenty of people who enjoy sissification *not* as a humiliating act but as a liberating expression of their own femininity. (Remember the story I told in chapter 2 about wimpy, the man who feels lovely in his panties?) For them, it's not humiliating at all. When they get sissified they want to be called a pretty little girl and do DIY manicures together. I have friends who are professional dominants who have a huge clientele of guys who want to dress as girls and just be pretty girls together. That's a *very* different kind of kink and self-expression than someone who *wants* to be mocked for being an ugly dude in a dress.

SISSY MAIDS

There's also a niche-within-a-niche community of sissies who enjoy the combination of frilly clothes and domestic service, so they might focus their identities or activities around being sissy maids. This can include all the traditional enjoyments of both categories, such as satin costumes and pink kink toys along with cleaning, assisting with getting dressed, and providing food and drink service. (More on domestic service play in chapter 15.)

SISSIFICATION IS NOT ONE SIZE FITS ALL

There are many different reasons someone might be compelled toward sissy play; finding the kernel of it is absolutely crucial because, again, you cannot humiliate someone with something they don't find humiliating. Sissification is very humiliating for some people and not humiliating at all for others. Men are often taught from a very young age that the worst possible thing you can be is a sissy. ("Sissy" and "slut," I think, are the two most gendered, intense insults that are used.) So, remember that, like any erotic humiliation activity, sissification play has to be tailored to the submissive's actual desires and preferences. The attraction to sissification, like I said, is often that men come seeking an experience that they've never had but have observed happening to others. They saw the way that a pretty girl in a dress became an object of desire or the locus of jealousy. They saw the display of prettiness as the red cape that a matador waves in front of a bull, and they decided that being the cape was more fun than being the bull. The same principals may or may not apply for any man—or anyone anywhere on the gender spectrum. (If you're looking for inspiration for sissification play, check out the Sissy Truth or Dare Deck in the resources section at the back of this book.)

Note that, while it's technically only sissification when a "man" is dressed and made to act like a "woman," we can achieve similar results across the gender spectrum by dressing anyone as close to the opposite of their self-image as possible. Treat them accordingly, and watch their cheeks redden and their genitals flush. My tomboyish, gender-queer friend hates being put in a dress. That's (socially speaking) what she's supposed to comfortably wear, but she finds it horribly humiliating. If you put her in a Lolita dress, she experiences the same loss of identity and frustration as a feminized man.

MORE WAYS TO PLAY

- The submissive is sent to a nail salon to get a mani/pedi in feminine colors.

- The submissive is assigned self-pampering days: bubble baths, freshly shaved legs, and DIY pedicures.

- The dom gets high heels for the sub to practice walking in and has them strut like models and/or balance books on their head.

- Wearing lingerie, the submissive dances like a stripper for their dom.

- The dominant uses makeup to make their submissive look "slutty."

- The submissive practices curtsies and feminine movement—bonus points if done in public.

- The submissive dresses entirely in women's clothing, and the dom points out how they *don't* look female.

- The dom has the submissive speak in feminized voices, then talk over them like most men do to women.

- Wearing a French maid outfit, the submissive cleans the house or otherwise serves their dom.

- The dominant waxes their submissive's bikini line, eyebrows, etc. Beauty is pain!

CHAPTER 13

NAKED IN FRONT OF THE CLASS: THE POWER OF TOTAL EXPOSURE

I dated a submissive who enjoyed being collared and led around her apartment and photographed. The pictures were never shared (or even taken off the camera) but the feeling that she could be exposed for having such fantasies created a real rush for her.

- FOOT REST BOY

NUDITY IS THE HUMAN BODY'S natural state, but most people, at least in the United States, feel very unnatural about it because our culture has told us it's wrong. This "wrongness" makes nudity an ideal playground for humiliation, influenced very much by the idea that only immodest and inferior people show off their bodies. The fact that inappropriate nudity is a super common stress dream is an indication of the power of exposure. It's literally something our subconscious tortures us with, and in erotic humiliation, we bring it into our conscious world. (If you come from a culture that doesn't create so much shame and judgment about the naked body, then this type of play may not pack the same punch.)

Inspecting the submissive's body and marking down measurements and responses is a classic way to bring attention to a person's physical self and get them feeling keenly uncomfortable in their own skin. As you inspect every inch of them, feel free to pinch, poke, and make comments ranging from lecherous to derogatory to disgusted. You can even make notes in a notebook or on a notepad on a clipboard for use later (or just to make them wonder what you could possibly be writing). It's important to remember here that many people grew up absorbing a great deal of shame about their bodies, and so a great deal of careful negotiation is necessary before you play on that shame (more on this later). Once you've established absolute trust, though, their naked body is your vulnerable canvas.

There are small ways to induce the vulnerability and availability of nudity. A common way to do this is to have your sub go underwear-free in public. While this is not likely to get you into too much trouble unless it involves an extremely short skirt and a windy day (no matter the gender of your sub), I recommend caution. Don't do anything that will get you or your plaything arrested. I always recommend people focus on the excitement of the *possibility* that someone might find out without actually doing something obscene that puts your livelihood at risk. After all, anticipation is much more exciting than jail time. But you can command them to go commando and give this a try.

If actual exposure is more enticing than mere risk, then public kink/sex parties can be a perfect and welcoming place to show off a naked submissive. This is a great opportunity to parade your sub around on a leash, showing off their naked-ness for all to see. Bonus points if you get people to objectify, laugh at, or (perhaps worse) completely ignore them (again, remember what I said about playing with body shame: care-ful negotiation is required). You'll get the effect of a public place without the pesky drawbacks of real-life consequences.

I'm personally a big fan of clothing choices that accentu-ate the awareness of one's own nudity and its (gasp!) inap-propriateness. For example, pulling someone's pants and underwear down around their ankles or strapping them into a leather harness that frames their bare nipples are ways to intensify the feeling of exposure.

It can be great fun and a significant exchange of power to take pictures/make videos of a nude person. Be careful to do this via analog or digital means *without* automatic backup protocols so that they can be summarily deleted and nobody has to worry. Unless, of course, the leverage of nudes is part of your play. If that's a dynamic you're using, proceed with caution, only play with trusted partners, and give up the idea of ever running for office.

Another fun activity to do with a nude sub is drawing on their body. You can use makeup, washable markers, or even permanent markers. You can write degrading names and terms like, "Disobedient Slut Slave" or, "Cum Dumpster." You can indicate instructions like, "Insert Dicks Here" or, "For Public

Use." You can even draw pictures on the nude body, just like friends sometimes draw dicks on an unconscious friend to humiliate them in the morning. That works on almost anyone. Bonus points for public exhibition in a safe and kinky environment.

Body image issues can be manipulated for this kind of humiliation play. However, play with caution. This field is full of especially sensitive land mines, and the distance between erotic humiliation and total disaster is shorter than most people think.

> I remember one guy spent months writing to me about how he couldn't wait to have me humiliate him and how he fantasized about me mocking his small dick. When he finally came in for the session, I started laying into him right away. "Your tiny little pencil dick is useless!" Within minutes, he was sobbing. Not cathartic sobbing, but holy shit just falling apart. "I have a small dick," he sobbed and couldn't even catch his breath. Suddenly, it wasn't fun for either of us anymore, because I'm not actually a sociopath, and he wasn't having the exciting time he had imagined. I stopped the scene, sat down, and talked about how sometimes fantasies need to stay in our mind. Sometimes the intensity of an action can turn out to be far less fun or much more emotionally difficult than we thought it would be. For years, this man had thought he wanted an intensely humiliating body-shaming scene, but it turned out to be a very sensitive topic.

The contrast between a naked submissive and a clothed dominant is a powerful one. People are always aware of the advantages someone nearby holds over them; being naked around clothed people makes a person very in tune with their vulnerability.

One popular type of porn and kink dynamic described as "Clothed Female, Naked Male" (CFNM) is a codified version of that phenomenon. Some subs have a really powerful response anytime you emphasize their nudity with your own non-nudity. However, not all subs find comparative exposure humiliating. I once knew a female submissive who would wear skirts in public and tuck the fabric of the skirt carefully into the waistband of her panties or her pantyhose. People would always try to help and discreetly tell her about it, but she had done it on purpose and didn't want it fixed. She wanted to be precariously exposed and did not find it humiliating in the least. Perhaps a little embarrassing, but also empowering.

On the other side of the coin, I had a male sub whom I would command to stand naked in the corner while my clothed friends and I sat around and had a conversation. He was humiliated beyond belief, and hopelessly turned on, just by being naked around clothed people.

I love making inspections of a submissive's nude body. I like to take the mad scientist approach. One of my theatrical BDSM props is a little clipboard with a small, yellow notepad on it. It looks very official. With this in hand, I make the submissive stand with their feet spread wide apart and their hands behind their neck. Depending on what their comfort level is, sometimes I make them look at the ground instead of at me to give them a little bit of buffer. Sometimes, I make them look me right in the eye, because that tends to make them feel more exposed and intense. I'll start fiddling with their bits, getting a read on their body as if evaluating it. I'll play with their nipples and say, "Oh, nipples seem to be work-ing...excellent," and then jot down some notes. The submis-sive inevitably gets nervous and asks, "What are you writing?" But the Princess never tells!

There is almost nothing more humiliating for many, many people than being asked to stand, bend over, and spread their ass cheeks. It's an *ass-toundingly* vulnerable position because the anus has so much cultural shame and taboo that just being forced to flash it can be powerfully humili-ating in all the right ways. With the right verbal play, it can evoke images of prison and captivity, of a life of no auton-omy or privacy, possibly even sexual coercion. Ask for that and watch horror dawn on someone's face...followed by lust.

For some people, reclaiming powerful words from real-life trauma around body image can provide an intense expe-rience of erotic humiliation. But I have to tell you, this is edgy and difficult play, and not for the faint of heart.

> My first exposure to erotic humiliation was just this type of play. I was a stripper at the time, and I had gone to a photographer to get some promotional photos done. At the end of the photo shoot, he asked me, "Do you want to see my dungeon down-stairs?" I said, "Yes! Absolutely!...I mean yes, that'd be lovely." He took me down to the dungeon and showed me around the extensive basement play-space. He said, "Do you want to see a video of my submissive?" I said, "Um, also yes." I tried to play it cool, but I'm too earnest to play it cool. I had never even seen a dungeon before, and I was thrilled with the possibilities.

So he turned on a video of a large-bodied woman kneeling in a bathtub, holding a five gallon paint bucket full of pee. As she poured the bucket of pee over her own head she chanted, "It is a pig. It is a toilet. It is a worthless slut. It is a pig. It is a toilet. It is a worthless slut." I was like, "Oh, wait. This is not at all what I imagined." Then she got dressed, putting the clothes on over the piss, and she put a sign on her back that read, "It is a fat toilet." She looked straight into the camera and said, "This fat pig toilet will now go walk around the mall for an hour, Master. Thank you for the privilege."

I admit, I was shaken; I had to stop and say, "Okay, can we talk about this?" As a feminist and a body-positive advocate, I was horrified. The photographer explained to me that they had had a very serious negotiation experience wherein the woman explained that for the majority of her life, people had told her body-normative garbage like, "You'd be so pretty if you would only lose weight," and, "You have such a pretty face." Then they would call her a cow behind her back. For her, it was this traumatic experience that she wanted to recontextualize, because with her consent and her control, she could assert power over how this happened and how she felt about it.

So, he would look her in the face and say, "You are a fat fucking cow, and I can't wait to fuck you!" He helped her to recontextualize it enough to make it into an erotic experience for her. This was a powerfully cathartic experience for this particular submissive, but is this kind of work something that you should launch into unannounced and hope that your sub will just...come around? Fuck no.

NOT-QUITE-NUDITY

There are also subtle ways to play with exposure (or potential exposure) by instructing the submissive to unbutton an extra button, unzip a back-zip skirt, or (for penis owners) wear shorts that are two sizes too tight.

This creates a lighter form of exposure and a softer experience that's more about potential embarrassment and risk than actual nudity. While most of this chapter is about getting someone naked and then making fun of them for it, not-quite-nudity is more about creating that exhilarating fear of, "Will someone see the outline of my junk through these shorts?" or, "Am I going to have a nip slip?" Just think of the backlash Janet Jackson (but not Justin Timeberlake?!) received after her infamous Super Bowl halftime show, and you'll understand what this lighter exposure play threatens.

When you're playing with nudity, from total exposure to the tiniest peekaboo, the moral of the story is this: talk about what feels sexy and humiliating and what creates the feeling you're trying to evoke. What are the emotional goals? Keep your eyes on the prize, get at the emotional kernel of how nudity feels, and then play it like a fiddle.

MORE WAYS TO PLAY

- The dom does a physical "inspection" of the sub, focusing on the feeling of exposure.
- The naked submissive stands as "art" while others have a meal or socialize around them.

- The submissive wears nipple clamps with bells (on nipples or genitalia) to emphasize nudity.

- Both players Google dance instruction videos from the '80s, and the dom watches as the submissive, either naked or in revealing clothing, attempts to replicate the dance moves.

- The dom rents a hotel room on a really high floor of a hotel and has the submissive stand naked in front of the window.

- The submissive is tied up with legs spread-eagle and put on "forced" display.

- The dominant makes a "no undies" rule for the house, so the submissive needs to remove their underwear immediately upon entering, and perhaps even hand them over to the dominant.

- The submissive does an exhibitionistic strip tease while the dominant throws coins, dollars, or crumpled paper at them.

CHAPTER 14

THINGS THAT MAKE YOU GO EWWW: PUTTING BODILY FUNCTIONS TO GOOD USE

And i let Her Piss fill my mouth until She says "swallow"
and allows me to take Her Pee inside me.

- L G

USING BODILY FUNCTIONS AND FLUIDS in humiliation play depends a lot on the "ick factor." Most of us are socialized to believe that some bodily functions (if not all) are seen as impolite, rude, or disgusting. These things are to be done in private, if at all. To incorporate these things into humiliation play, we can use the social repulsion factor, the power of "forcing" someone to endure the grossness of the actions, and/or the emphasis on their desire for these "gross" activities. There are many ways to play with bodily fluids, one of the most common being "golden showers" or piss play.

PISS PLAY

What's the appeal of piss play? It's a very versatile activity, ranging from sensuous and sexual to degrading and humiliating. The sensations of piss play are both physical and psychological. Coming straight from a person, piss is warm. Depending on how much you can control your flow, it can either be light, slow drips or it can be a torrential rain. Psychologically, it can be like marking territory in a primal way for the dominant and being marked as property for the submissive. It can make you both feel sensual. It can be humiliating for the submissive and empowering for the dominant. There's great variety that can be created with the energy of the scene and the vocabulary used.

A common assumption is that all piss play is done with one person doing the peeing and another person receiving the pee, but another popular way to play is to have the submissive wet themselves, either naked or clothed. This is called "Omorashi" or "Desperate Wetting" and involves the individual becoming desperate and "accidentally" wetting themselves. Wetting oneself can feel erotic, taboo, humiliating, playful, and so much more, and doing so can be a form of submission or even brattiness.

SAFETY

Like in every kind of play, communication is crucial in piss play. But because this involves an exchange of body fluids, there are some specific safety issues you need to remain aware of. For an overview of the health issues with safe piss play, I've asked my good friend Dr. Brian to share his expertise.

Dr. Brian is a doctor, but he is not your doctor. While his advice here is golden, please do not take it as a medical endorsement of your particular play scenarios, but reach out to your doctor with specific questions and concerns about your personal situation.

DR. BRIAN'S PISS SAFETY ESSAY

Many people like to play with urine in a BDSM setting. Golden showers and human toilet training inevitably lead to questions about the safety of imbibing pee. The way that urine is formed in the kidneys is interesting. Your kidneys clean your blood in a way that would be like someone coming into your house, removing every bit of furniture and decoration, and then putting them back, minus the garbage you didn't want. I could go on and on about the kidneys and the urinary tract, but that's what nephrologists are for, and I'm a mere general practitioner.

Urine is funneled to the bladder from the kidneys by means of two smaller tubes, the ureters. It is stored in the bladder until it is socially acceptable to be eliminated. Of course, in most settings, the "socially acceptable" receptacle is a toilet, but in other settings, it's a slave's mouth. Whatever the target, urine is transported from the bladder by way of the urethra out of the body.

The major component of urine is overwhelmingly water. Anywhere from 95 to 99 percent of urine will be water, based on the hydration status of the person making it. This is intuitive, and I'm not telling you anything you don't know. On a hot day after you exercise, your urine is darker, but after you chug lots and lots of water, it's clear. There are several other components of urine. Urea is a byproduct of protein metabolism through which the body excretes nitrogen. In fact, urine was processed in the past (think Revolutionary War) to make a major component of gunpowder. Every liter of urine contains more than nine grams of urea. Similarly, a liter of urine contains one gram of sodium and three-quarters of a gram of potassium. There are several other solutes, like creatinine, in smaller amounts. The component of urine that makes it yellow is urobilinogen, which is a byproduct of the breakdown of hemoglobin contained in red blood cells. There is a fair amount of solute in urine, and there are better ways to quench your thirst.

Urine is theoretically sterile, as anyone who has seen *Dodgeball* knows. That is, it is sterile when it is formed, but by the time it gets to the bladder, it is no longer entirely sterile. Certainly by the time it passes through a person's urethra, it contains minor amounts of bacteria. This is true even in a healthy individual. There is some risk of disease transmission with urine ingestion, but the risk is relatively low. HIV is not transmitted by urine, and contracting hepatitis B through urine is theoretically possible but not very likely. There are other pathogens that reside in urine and can potentially be transmitted, but again, the rates of transmission are low. There have been some studies recently that show Sars-CoV-2 (COVID 19) is present in urine. As a precaution, wasting the first bit of a urine stream makes sense and is a good practice when serving it up. Similarly, physicians' offices ask patients to collect the mid-stream of urine for their specimens. This allows the first portion of the stream to wash out bacteria and debris from the urethra and ensures that the sample is representative of the urine in the bladder. This is the so-called "clean catch" and should reduce the number of potential pathogens in a urine sample. Urine play with women during menstruation is more problematic when it comes to disease transmission. During periods of heavy menstrual flow, it is possible for urine to be contaminated with blood. This will potentially increase the number of pathogens that can infect someone who comes in contact with it and will also increase the efficiency of transmission. It should be avoided unless a pair is **fluid bonded**.

Urine consumption has been practiced by many cultures for cosmetic and health purposes, and it is used today in an alternative medicinal practice called "urine therapy." Currently, however, there is a lack of medical evidence for the benefits of urine therapy. The amount of solute in urine also means that it is not advisable to drink as an alternate fluid source when water is not available. For this reason, survival manuals published by the Army advise against drinking urine as a survival technique. The urban legend that, on a lifeboat, everyone should pee in the water supply to increase it may sound fun to the human urinals out there, but it's not good practice, healthwise. The occasional ingestion of urine, however, will not result in dehydration. The sodium and solute load of urine can be diluted by having the person producing the urine drink water prior to urinating and by having the person ingesting it drink water shortly after imbibing. It should also not be ingested in great quantities or exclusively, or it will certainly lead to dehydration, but the occasional golden cocktail isn't going to harm a submissive.

There are several medications that have active metabolites that are excreted in urine and could potentially have an effect on someone ingesting them. Similarly, the ingestion of vitamins, supplements, and minerals can impact the composition of urine. It's a well-known fact that asparagus will give urine a distinctive odor. It is a lesser-known fact that artificial sweeteners are excreted in urine and will give it a sweeter taste.

Urine by itself is caustic. Urine left in contact with the skin for extended periods of time will result in skin breakdown, and incontinence is a predisposition for the development of bed sores in patients. Along the same lines, subjects that have sensitive skin can develop a rash when their skin comes in contact with urine. Urine in the eye can be an irritant, but the more serious risk is when a person is infected with gonorrhea, meaning their urine is infectious. Their urine could cause an eye infection and result in keratoconjunctivitis, which is a condition that, if left untreated, will result in blindness. This isn't a subtle infection; it causes a faucet of drainage from the eyes. The simplest precaution to avoid these complications is to wash off and irrigate the eye with saline solution as soon as practical.

Finally, just a quick word about scat and coprophagia, or eating poop. It's not recommended. Eating another person's stool is risky and could result in viral infections such as Hepatitis A, hepatitis E, or polio. There are any number of bacterial infections that will result from this infection, most notably E. coli. Intestinal parasites such as amebiasis, roundworms, and giardia can also be transmitted via poop. There have been studies completed during the pandemic that demonstrate Sars-CoV-2 (COVID 19) is present in stool and infectious. Ultimately, however, there will be some that engage in this practice. The most effective way to avoid contracting some rather serious illnesses is to know your partner, ensure that they are healthy, and avoid ingesting anything that is grossly contaminated with blood.

LIMITS

It is imperative to be able to talk about your limits before playing with bodily functions. For example, you should have an honest conversation about drinking piss. Some people do not want to ingest it at all, some people want to be "forced" to drink it (again, there's that consensual non-consent concept), and some want it full-face/mouth-wide-open, drinking it up like a greedy piss slut! However, there are plenty of ways to enjoy piss play without ingestion. You don't need to require your submissive to swallow when it can be powerful enough just to bathe in it.

THE LOGISTICS

As even the experienced pisser can tell you, piss play can be messy. Do your best to contain the piss in the first place, and cleanup will be a lot easier for everybody. Think about your container and its seal. If you're on a bed, do you have waterproof sheets or a doggy pad beneath you? Think about how absorbent the floor is—can you do this on tile? A bathroom is, of course, the best place for simple cleanup, if not for comfort.

Cleanup is when power dynamics can come in very handy for a dominant. After a golden shower session, I just tell my submissive to clean it up!

If you frequently engage in piss play, invest in a stock of large plastic garbage bags, puppy pee-training pads, plastic tarps, or small inflatable summer pools (get them at the dollar store or Kmart). After play, you can just wrap up the materials covered in piss and put them in a large plastic garbage bag to put in the trash. If you do it in a shower or bath or over the toilet, then cleanup is super easy—just rinse! If any does leak on carpet, use a cleaner that you've already tried on a hidden piece to see what the results will be like. Most urine won't damage fabric or carpet, but it is possible the dye will be affected, and the smell can be very difficult to remove.

PREPARATION

You should drink plenty of water to prepare for the session, but the amount and the rate of consumption depends on your body. If you know that you're going to be doing a golden shower session early in the day, try to hold it in the morning if you can to create the most torrential flow. If you're playing at the end of the day, drink water consistently and experiment with how comfortable you are, trying to hold it longer and longer before going to the bathroom. As it gets closer to playtime, see if you can wait and just keep holding it! A word of caution: Trying to hold it too long can easily lead to a urinary tract infection (UTI) or even a kidney infection. In extreme cases, the bladder can rupture. There is a difference between discipline and danger. Obey the urges of your body, but try to manipulate your comfort.

There are some ways to control the taste and smell of your piss. Broccoli and asparagus are classics; if you eat a large serving of either, your pee will turn bright green and will be incredibly sour and strong-smelling. Coffee creates a bitter taste, and B12 vitamins make the color bright orange.

MORE WAYS TO PLAY WITH PISS

- The submissive lies in the bathtub with their head down and ass up, holding open their ass cheeks so the dom can "shoot for the hole."

- The dom puts the sub in a tub or a small kiddie pool and leaves them there for a period of time, pissing on them throughout the day/night.

- The submissive wears a funnel-gag for "forced" ingestion (check out Stockroom.com for a quality option).

- The dom chooses a special glass or container that is used just for the submissive to drink the dom's golden nectar.

- The dom makes the sub piss their pants by tickling or denying them access to the bathroom.

- The dom puts the submissive in a diaper and pees into it (or makes them pee in it).

- The dom pisses into a dog dish and makes the submissive drink from it like a dog.

- The dom pisses into their own underwear, takes them off, and slaps the sub with them. Or makes a tasty gag!

- The submissive is allowed to watch the dom closely while they pee.

- The submissive cleans the dom after they've pissed, acting as "human toilet paper."

- The dom pees into a measuring cup and has the submissive guess the volume. If sub is correct, they get to drink it; if not, it gets dumped on their head.

OTHER BODILY FLUIDS AND FUNCTIONS

SPIT

Spit's great. Spit is definitely one of those things that you may feel spontaneous about playing with, but saliva can be an emotional or physical trigger, so it's something you want to negotiate first. Genuine spitting can feel very spontaneous. You'll just suddenly go "Puh-*tooie*!" and it's so empowering! But if there hasn't been some discussion of playing with spit, and specifically spitting in their face, and you do it noncon-sensually, your sub may never speak to you again. Spitting is another one of those things that can be an unexpectedly big trigger for people for reasons of trauma or cultural context. To ramp up slowly, you can put a little spit on your finger and then wipe it on their cheek. It's not as forceful but can be a great way to introduce a submissive to spit play.

One way to make it fun is to use a washable marker or lipstick to make a target on the body of the submissive and try spitting to hit the target. Make sure to keep water nearby to stay hydrated!

You'll be surprised at how many different kinds of ways to spit there are, and where, as the dominant, you might draw the line. After all, we all have limits.

For example, personally I love to give a good sponta-neous, impetuous "Puh-*tooie*" right in my submissive's face—derisive, almost dismissive. But I don't personally like hocking up loogies, even if it is a great way to get to total disgust very quickly. Not that it's beyond me or something. I grew up in the country, so spitting was basically a sport when I was a kid. I can hock a loogie pretty much anytime, but I gag think-ing about hocking a loogie in someone's face. The idea of somebody swallowing boogers and spit grosses me out too much. I can't help but think, "Oh no, honey, get that out of your mouth. Get it out of your mouth."

Of course, spitting on genitals is usually pretty popular, whether during sex or other types of kinky play. It's a great way to express disgust. Bonus points for combining this with word play—calling someone "slut" and "whore" while spitting on their filthiest bits will make them feel used and demeaned in the sexiest sort of way!

Don't forget, spitting is still a fluid exchange, so don't do it without specific consent and a safer sex conversation.

SWEAT AND OTHER SMELLY FUNCTIONS

Scent is one of our strongest senses. The memories that scents trigger can be extremely intense. The scents themselves—the pheromones—can be sensual on their own, but they can also invoke a great sense of cultural shame for some people. I got very into scent play toward the end of my professional dominatrix career. I trained my submissives and clients to fetishize me sweaty and wearing sweatpants, because I had grown tired of fetish clothing and had developed a kink for comfort. It was like, "We're going to do a smelly session because I just don't care to take a shower for you. Sniff away, you slut."

Smelly feet is one of the most popular manifestations of foot fetish, though there's an important distinction between a foot fetishist who specifically enjoys smelly *feet* (though not necessarily other smelly things) and a humiliation fetishist who's turned on by many smelly things, including feet. (If you relate more to the former than the latter, check out the whole chapter about feet earlier in the book.)

Armpit smelling is a particularly popular scent fetish, particularly in gay male dynamics. Sometimes this is simply erotic, but forcing someone to smell your armit can also be an exciting humiliation tool.

Farting is a bodily function that can be really fun and a bit silly. When I fart for my submissives, I like to make it super dramatic. They have to kneel behind me and sniff loudly and clap for me after I fart in their face. It's also an excellent humiliating addition to "queening," where you sit on their face as breath play and then fart with their nose between your ass cheeks.

It depends on your own body chemistry, but you can help create gas by eating a plate of beans or broccoli. It can be fun to make them watch you eat it to create a sense of antic-ipation. Or you can just capitalize when spontaneous farting occurs. "Come quick, Princess has to fart!"

You can also embarrass your submissive in public by tuck-ing a remote control gag-gift type farting machine into the back of their pants and setting it off when someone walks nearby. Embarrassing, silly fun!

CUM

Making someone eat their own cum is also a very popular body fluid activity. All along the gender spectrum, people have very distinct feelings about the juices from their genita-lia. If you're playing with someone who has a penis and they ejaculate before they're allowed (or even on command), by all means feed it to them—or make them wear it by smearing it all over their body. Many people have internalized shame about the smell of their genitals. If you are finger fucking someone with a vagina and they are really embarrassed by the idea of "pussy smell," making them sniff and lick their own pussy juices will be an embarrassing, humiliating act.

But the response might not always be so reticent. There are some lovely sluts that you'll finger fuck and they'll be like,"Oh yeah. I want to slurp it up! Yeah!" You want to make sure the response you're looking for is the response you're going to get. You can be saying, "Yeah, these are your dirty sex juices," with the intent of mortifying your sub, but if they respond enthusiastically—"Yes! Give it all to me!"—you may find yourself with someone cock-gobbling your finger and choking themselves on their own clit jam.

MORE WAYS TO PLAY WITH CUM

- The dom spreads cum all over the submissive's body and, after it dries, makes them put clothes on over it to go out into the world.

- The dom saves cum (in a shot glass in the freezer, for example) and then puts it into a smoothie the sub has to drink.

- Before sending them out into the world, the dom cums on the sub's face and lets it dry.

- The sub is made to cum onto their own body or in their own face.

- The sub is commanded to lick the cum off of a shoe, boot, or the floor.

- The dom cums on a dildo and then use it for blow-job training.

- Using dedicated plates, the sub is made to eat salad with cum for dressing.

CHAPTER 15

THE BUTT-PLUGGED BUTLER: DOMESTIC SERVICE AND CLEANING

I had a female roommate that found the easiest way to keep peace of mind was to have a set of rules with consequences. For example, if I wasn't keeping up with my half of the chores, I would have to spend a Saturday wearing a "cleaning" uniform (usually a dress and panties underneath). One of her pet peeves was me peeing on the toilet seat. After a couple of warnings I was punished by having to ask permission to pee for a week, which was either supervised or I was told to squat like a girl to avoid the seat.

- M

FOR MANY, BEING FORCED TO act as a servant, with a focus on cleaning or domestic activities, works well within a humiliation dynamic. There are a number of ways to incorporate an element of service into your play.

Cleaning in and of itself can be a humiliating act. Many men consider it to be "women's work," so they feel inferior for being made to vacuum, dust, or do dishes. Emphasizing the misogyny of this outlook is a great place to start for that sort of player. There's also a classist perspective on cleaning, so many people experience a class-based social shame around having to take care of such domestic chores.

If you are going to have somebody clean, whoever it is, you can have them do it naked or in a sexy/funny costume. Turn them into a pirate and have them scrub your grout! Put them in high heels and an overly sexualized outfit and make them clean and tidy the living room. Bonus points if you have guests over who can appreciate the service being provided! Or make the submissive wear a spreader bar between their legs or wrists so they're hobbled in their movements (think Maggie Gyllenhaal stapling office paperwork in *Secretary*). Nipple or genital clamps with bells on them are a great way to emphasize their nudity and movement as they clean.

There's a creative product on the market by Scott Paul Designs called the Humiliator Gag. It's a mouth gag with a specialized joint for attaching items such as a toilet brush, ash tray, or feather duster. With a simple click, you can change out the attachment according to the task at hand.

But if you're going to have the submissive clean, then have them *really* clean—this is not just playtime! Give the areas that have been cleaned the white glove test; if something isn't clean enough, they have to do it again, and preferably in a *more* humiliating outfit or in a more disgusting and humiliating manner (licking a surface clean or using a tooth-brush works nicely here). I used to leave little notes in places that they weren't likely to remember to clean, like behind the toilet. I would leave a little note that said, "If you find this, bring it to Me for the privilege of placing one kiss on My ass." They would hardly ever find it, because they didn't get that far in their cleaning.

Inspecting the submissive's work should also be an important part of the session. You don't have to do it every time, but the submissive must know that you *might* do it, so they should always be expecting it. At least during the first few cleaning sessions, you should do a thorough inspection to give instructional feedback and check their ability levels. Then, you might suddenly stop doing the inspections for two weeks before resuming spontaneously. Do it at your whim and leisure. The submissive should learn to check every detail, every time, according to your standards, for fear that you might inspect, and for fear of the (erotically humiliating) consequences.

Keeping a house clean is an ongoing process and can be a structured assignment or an occasional assistance. You can make a list of the daily, weekly, or monthly cleaning tasks that need to be done in order of priority. Then, explain exactly how you like things to be done—this is the only way you can be assured things will be done to your standards, and it reinforces the looming threat of inspection. Stand over your submissive the first few times they have to scrub the toilet. The idea of being watched doing such a demeaning task is humiliating in itself; the idea of being watched *and* judged is mortifying.

Doing laundry is usually a very personal task, so if you're going to grant your submissive the honor of doing this for you, it's even more important that you go over your style and needs. You can teach your submissive to use the proper soaps, fold your clothes to your specifications, put them away in the correct places, iron and mend your clothes, and even polish your shoes. The teaching can carry the threat of further humiliation and punishment for doing it wrong. Allowing the submissive to take notes here is a way to set them up for success, while making them memorize your instructions can be an added layer of difficulty and a fun part of the test.

As usual, make sure you're on the same page about the goal of a domestic service exchange. Are you really looking to have the cleaning be effective, or is it more for the humiliation? I have definitely found that a lot of the requests I got from new cleaning subs were more about the humiliation than the final product. They'd scrub one spot over and over while saying, "Princess, I'm cleaning. Princess, I'm cleaning. Princess. Princess, I'm cleaning for you. Princess, I'm cleaning for you." I'd respond, "No, really you're not. You've just worn the tile down in that one spot in my kitchen." Make sure that you're very clear on what your expectations are if you want the cleaning to be competent.

SERVICE BEYOND CLEANING

House chores are far from the only way to offer service. Another popular form of service-based humiliation play is about turning the submissive into a party servant who offers not only table-side service for food and drink, but also entertainment for guests through playful or stern expectations.

I had the opportunity to serve a dinner party with my wife and two other women while I was dressed as a maid. There were games I had no chance of

*winning that I would receive a punishment for los-
ing as well as a punishment for each error made
while serving. The punishments were pies in the
face, spanking and forced foot worship. It was the
most fun I've ever had.*

- SploshLover

As a dominant who has had multiple submissives act as domestic servants, I can personally attest to how much fun this kind of play can be—and how much fun it is to always have a clean house and never have to do your own laundry. Just be sure you're both approaching this with your kernel kinks in mind so you don't lose sight (like I did in the story I told about my domestic servant in chapter 6) of ensuring a satisfying experience for both of you.

MORE WAYS TO PLAY

- The dom ties rags or sponges to the submissive's breasts or genitals to use for scrubbing.

- The submissive uses a toothbrush or very small scrubber for attention to detail.

- The sub is required to lick and taste the difference between a dirty and clean surface.

- The dominant sticks trash on the submissive's body and punishes them if any falls on the clean floor.

- Immediately after the sub cleans up an area, the dom makes a mess by spitting out food, walking through with dirty shoes, etc.

- The dom incorporates verbal humiliation/degradation play by comparing the submissive to the mildew in the tub, scum around the toilet bowl, etc.

- The dom completely ignores the submissive while they clean, emphasizing the fact that they are relaxing and enjoying themself in any number of ways while the submissive labors away cleaning.

CHAPTER 16

THIS IS FOR YOUR OWN GOOD: PUNISHMENT AND PROTOCOL

I like humiliating someone for their own good.
I am a punishment fetishist and humiliation is a
uge part of facing one's mistakes while someone
discusses them openly, having your errors pointed
out and corrected, and submitting to and enduring
punishment to reach redemption and forgiveness
(and I am turned on just typing this).

- S

I GROUP PUNISHMENT and **PROTOCOL** under the larger heading of discipline, but in reality, they're two topics that are distinct yet related.

Protocol: Rules for how certain things should be done, such as how a submissive should stand or how they should speak when spoken to.

Punishment: For behavior modification (and frequently, just for fun, a.k.a. "funishment!").

PROTOCOL

Protocol is shorthand for the social rituals you want your submissive to follow. This might include how you expect your sub to greet you (titles they use or actions they take), how you want them to address other people (as equals, superiors, etc.), how they should leave or enter a room, where or how they should stand, how they should behave at public events, whether or when eye contact is appropriate, if they are allowed on furniture, how they should refer to themselves (I, it, this sub, Your sub, etc.), and how they communicate.

The most complicated (and often most fun) protocols to establish tend to be physical positions. Popular positions:

- Kneeling with head down and forehead pressed against the floor
- Kneeling with head up and hands behind their back or neck
- Standing at attention
- Nose to the wall
- Various sexually available positions.

Learning how to hold still while in these "slave" positions takes concentration and practice. Being still and attentive teaches body awareness as well as "active waiting," which can be a very important skill for a service submissive.

MORE WAYS TO PLAY WITH PROTOCOL

- The submissive practice positions through a type of kinky Simon Says game.
- The submissive wears a leash and collar to learn to heel as they walk behind the dominant.
- The dom uses impact play to distract the sub as they practice positions.
- The submissive is instructed to practice tone of voice and facial expressions in a mirror.

PUNISHMENT

The arbitrary way a dominant dishes out punishment can be a great way to underscore a power dynamic. The dominant can assign punishment based on actual mistakes to spark behavior modification (but never *ever* punish a submissive from a place of real anger!) or merely for their own pleasure and amusement.

In terms of habit building, people are like dogs. For the most part, if you do not punish a behavior you want to change immediately after it occurs, the habit will not change. So when you set up a punishment, it has to be something realistic and efficient. As an example, if a submissive says a word/ phrase/title that is not allowed and the dominant responds with, "You've screwed up. You're not going to get to cum for ten months," is that realistic? Probably not. Is it connected to the undesirable behavior? Not at all. Punishment must be directly associated with the way it was earned and the behavior we want to change. Perhaps immediately washing the submissive's mouth out with soap would be a more effective punishment. We're back to Pavlov here. Make the bell symbolize food, and the association will last; make the punishment inspire proper behavior, and *that* association will last.

> *Goal setting has become a new favorite of mine. Making my pet set goals for herself and then holding her accountable is potentially both empowering and self-sabotaging predicament play. Since she sets the goals, she has only herself to blame if/ when she fails.*
>
> *- Father Klyde*

TYPES OF PUNISHMENT

People get very humiliated by being treated like children or being disciplined. Some submissives seek to relinquish a strong element of control; for example, some want their bathroom privileges controlled, and some want to be forbidden to use furniture or to have their speech restricted.

NOSE-TO-THE-WALL

This is a classic punishment that's reminiscent of old schoolhouses and naughty youngsters. However, it can get boring for the sub if there isn't another layer added. Put them in the corner with their pants around their ankles or their skirt tucked up to show off their ass. Or pour rice on the floor for them to kneel on. As something more actionable, force them to hold a quarter or "punishment point" against the wall with their nose (bonus points if you secure their hands behind their back!).

Even then, if you've got somebody with their nose in the corner for twenty minutes, that can be a long stretch to stay aroused or even interested. To keep things exciting, I love to do what I call **active ignoring**. Every once in a while, I might just come over to where I have them positioned and say, "You need to get closer to the corner," and then walk away. It doesn't have to be a circus act interaction. It doesn't have to be a lengthy thing every single time. You don't have to hover over them for twenty minutes, although if you want to, you can. They're not going to be looking at you. Just the occasional scolding is enough to keep them interested. "Nose in the corner!"

WRITING SENTENCES

Writing sentences is another classic that really never goes out of style. If you screw up my laundry you're going to write, "I am a stinky sock sniffer," three hundred times—and in three different-colored pens so I know you didn't photocopy it! Force the sub to produce and prove an accurate count. Remind them that it is not your job to make sure they've copied correctly, so if you discover that the count is low, you'll add another page. One way to do that is to have them number each line so you can see it counting up.

CORPORAL PUNISHMENT

Physical discipline can also fall under humiliation for some people (and the next chapter is dedicated to just that!). Use corporal punishment, telling the submissive, "It's going to hurt, but it's for your own good." Or put them in a predicament such as having to hold up a heavy stack of books while they're stimulated and aroused.

Face slapping has come up in many of my workshops as a very degrading physical activity that can be used as punishment. It's an action that requires a good understanding of safety (the head is a delicate thing!), but it is incredibly intimate and intense. Two good rules to follow are to only use your fingers (never your palm) and to only strike on their cheek (not the whole face). Also, it doesn't take a lot of power to get your point across; this is not about swinging your arm and slapping them wildly. You're much better off using less force and relying on taboo and intimacy for the humiliation.

Figging is also a fun (and painful) option for physical punishment. Carve a piece of ginger into a butt plug by peeling the skin off and shaping it into a phallic shape. (Don't forget to make a flared base so it doesn't get lost inside of them!) Then require the submissive to hold the piece of ginger in with their ass cheeks while getting spanked or being put in the corner. The spiciness of the ginger causes a burning sensation that really ups the ante!

VERBAL SCOLDING

Lectures on discipline can be super hot for some and dreadful for others. Getting a verbal "dressing down" for a real or imagined slight can bring about feelings of being small and vulnerable and under the dominant's direction. Wag your finger, deny eye contact, or have the submissive look you square in the eye as you talk down to them. I've found that intelligence-based insults aren't well received by most people, but there are some subs who enjoy them. Just make sure you know which is which.

MORE WAYS TO PLAY WITH PUNISHMENT

- The submissive has to balance a book on their head while doing squats.
- The dominant washes the sub's mouth out with soap (use bar soap, not squirt soap).
- The submissive is forced to wear a dunce cap wear while doing chores.
- Exercise such as jumping jacks or sit-ups makes for healthy punishment!
- A cold shower can be an invigorating punishment.
- All meals for a set period of time must be foods the sub dislikes.
- The submissive wears a clothespin on their tongue if they've "talked back" or been rude.

CHAPTER 17

THWACKS, STINGS, SCRATCHES, AND SQUEALS: USING IMPACT AND SENSATION

I love combining impact and humiliation. They are two of my favorite kinds of play, so they overlap a lot for me. I feel like humiliation adds a lightness to heavy impact scenes. Laughter and joking help the endorphins come into play. Plus, you get to hit someone really hard and then laugh at them for showing that it hurts. How is that not fun?

- ELENA DE LUCA

IMPACT PLAY, LIKE BONDAGE (WHICH we'll discuss in the next chapter) is all about controlling another person's physical sensations. In the context of impact play, it's about creating a sense of overload that leads to discomfort. In traditional, non-humiliation-related impact play, this is generally limited to physical discomfort from flogging, etc.; however, when it comes to erotic humiliation and impact play, all senses are fair game— and so is a level of absurdity rarely seen in traditional impact play. If I want to make you listen to "Baby Shark" on loop for hours on end (with headphones of course, because there's no way I'm subjecting myself to that) while I spank you with a toy shark, I totally can.

But impact play doesn't have to be absurd to be humiliating. When we increase sensation in our bodies, that can help us tap into our emotions in a really powerful way. If I spank your ass until it's red, warm to the touch, and puffy, I'm exposing an intimate part of your body in a dramatic way. Similarly, many women enjoy having their breasts flogged, highlighting a hypersensitive part of the body and, in the process, making it even more sensitive. (Running your fingers lightly over a freshly beaten ass cheek produces a very different sensation than it would before the beating.) Other possibilities include "forced" masturbation with sandpaper, or stimulating any kind of genitals past the point of orgasm so the overstimulation is uncomfortable.

Uncomfortable is not the same thing as unsafe though, so let's touch on a few quick safety tips:

- Aim is more important than power! You don't have to (and shouldn't) swing from your shoulder to put your full strength behind the impact.

- There are many different types of impact and sensation, so carefully consider how each toy feels on the body—stingy, thuddy, scratchy, itchy—and whether that's the desire

- For impact play that includes striking someone, stick to the fleshy and broad parts of the body, such as the shoulders, buttocks, thighs, and chest. The face and genitals are also options but strike those with much less force.

- It's vitally important to avoid hitting the spine, kidneys, and major organ areas (including lower back and belly), as well as the shins, ears, and tops of the feet.

- Everyone's pain scale is different, so be sure that all parties understand what intensity level is desired and tolerable

Regardless of the specific method, the purpose of humiliation-based impact play is for the dominant to create physical discomfort for the sub—and then mock the shit out of them for it. As you're exploring adding impact play to your erotic humiliation menu, there are four key elements to consider.

1. WHICH TOOLS TO USE

In the non-humiliating BDSM world, impact play tools are often works of art—leather flogs, wooden paddles, etc.—used to inflict pain in a highly *aesthetic* way. And those are perfectly valid tools for humiliation, as well. For example, I used to love using those little hand crops—or really any crops—to hit people's buttholes. The tool was "artful" or "fancy," but the way I was using it—to just smack the (figurative!) shit out of someone's butthole—made it both very exposed and inti-mate and very humiliating for the sub.

Then again, in humiliation, you aren't limited to the "tra-ditional" tools. If you're into high-level absurdity, you can use items as ridiculous as you want. I've had a few friends over the years who've had particular proclivities for using rubber chickens for spankings and floggings.

Or, you can work with no tools at all. Even things like tick-ling—under the arms, on the sides, or even in the inner thighs and other erogenous zones or "private parts"—can cause powerful sensory overload and cause a sub to lose control, which is a humiliating feeling for sure.

When you're deciding which tools and toys to use, con-sider the specific sensation you're trying to evoke, and then identify the tools that will help you get there. Are you playing with gender? Then you might consider hitting your masculine sub with a lady's hair brush—or your foot fetishist sub with a man's smelly tennis shoe. Or maybe, for someone who isn't into sissification, consider running silky panties or even just a piece of silky satin over their body and then pointing out how turned on they're getting by such a feminine sensation.

If you want to explore cold play, consider exploring the coldness of latex (and capitalizing on the fact that it feels like a condom), freezing a stainless steel sex toy to insert while still frigid, or pelting them with ice. If you want to keep things hot, you can also do some wax play (soy candles are safest—don't use ones from the dollar store). You could even apply BenGay™, Icy Hot™, or Tiger Balm™ for those temperature sensations (although stay away from sensitive membranes like the genitals and eyes, because once you get it on, it's dif-ficult to get off, and the sensation can escalate quickly).

Your imagination (and your mutual consent) is the limit, so when it comes to tools and toys, feel free to get creative about what objects and materials will produce the desired result.

2. WHICH BODY PARTS TO HIGHLIGHT AND WHICH POSITIONS TO USE

Next, consider the different ways you can position a sub for maximum embarrassment.

While a typical BDSM spanking bench may be great for bringing pain alone, over-the-knee spanking is a particularly humiliating position. Just the thought of being ass-up, writhing against the dom's knee, kicking their feet, vulnerable and exposed, trying not to put all their weight on the dom while teetering precariously makes many subs flush with erotic shame. Bonus points for using your hands to pry their ass cheeks apart for an inspection or some teasing.

Another humiliating position is to have the sub grab their ankles and bend over. Ass up and butthole exposed is a great position for any impact implement, such as a paddle or cane. (If bodily ability prevents the sub from bending all the way over, having them lean over the top of a chair or couch, or even facedown on a bed or floor can also work.)

Finally, besides being a great punishment, face slapping is considered to be one of the most humiliating forms of impact play for multiple reasons, including the intimacy of being struck across the face as well as its perception as a contemptuous, dismissing, or demeaning action. It's also an incredibly risky way to play (I teach an entire class on it), so take particular care.

3. HOW THE SUB EXPRESSES AND RESPONDS TO PAIN

As always, verbal humiliation is a big part of creating the right emotional experience, even when we're focused on physical actions like impact and sensation exploration. When you mock them for the way they express their pain, that adds another delicious layer of humiliation to the play.

Note that different subs will receive pain in different ways, but no matter how they do it, there is *always* a way to mock them for it.

They may receive it badly, like my submissive wimpy does. In fact, that's how he got his name in the first place. The first time we did impact play together, he wiggled and squirmed and made these hilarious squeaking sounds. So I mocked him mercilessly for not being able to take the pain I wanted to dish out (and that he wanted me to dish out), and I've called him "wimpy" ever since.

On the other hand, a sub may be totally stoic, taking the pain in stride, barely flinching. If that's the case, it's a great opportunity to tell them how boring they are. "God, you're so boring! I'm whacking you with all of my might, and you're not even responding! It's like playing with a rock!" Or tell them what a loser they are. "You're so out of touch with your emotions that you just can't even express or respond to this incredible pain I'm dishing out."

Or, a sub who receives it badly at first may eventually change their tune: I've had multiple submissives who were originally disinterested in pain play but became curious and eager to explore it with me once they saw how much joy and glee I sparkle with after physically whooping someone's ass. Whenever I teased wimpy about "being such a wimp," he would grin with chagrin and then I would command him to "ask Me for another." Before we knew it, he was asking in earnest. And you already know my story of (consensually) zapping another sub's cock until he learned to beg for it with the proper level of enthusiasm—then continuing to zap it until he was begging for real.

When it comes to dishing out pain, a sub may be on either end of the spectrum or anywhere in between. Like I said, there's always a way to mock them for fun and pleasure. And if the sensation you're exploring isn't necessarily pain but arousal (like with the silky satin) or something else, mock them for how turned on (or whatever) they are by such an "inappropriate" sensation.

4. IS IT OKAY TO LEAVE MARKS?

When it comes to impact play (of the BDSM or erotic humiliation variety), marks—and whether it's okay to leave them on each other—are a polarizing topic. For some people, being black and blue feels liberating and is a source of pride. For others, it feels like walking around with a big old Scarlet Letter—the mark of the pervert.

Obviously, as with every facet of erotic humiliation, whether or not marks are okay is something you'll negotiate in advance, and if either player doesn't consent, then the dom does everything in their power to make sure not to leave any marks. But with the sub's consent, leaving marks can be another way to add to the embarrassment: "Look at these strikes on you! Everybody's gonna know you like this. Everybody's gonna know you're a dirty pervert." Even if you *talk* about leaving marks without actually leaving them, depending on what you've negotiated, highlighting that vulnerability and that potential exposure can be a powerful way to create erotic shame.

The physical sensations of impact play are, for many kinksters, tantalizing on their own. But add in an element of humiliation and (if you're like me) absurdity, and you can take this kind of play to a whole different level.

MORE WAYS TO PLAY

- The submissive bobs and weaves as the dominant pelts them with a Nerf™ gun, either by chasing them or by sitting in a chair as the submissive stands facing them.

- On a day when the submissive will be out in the sun in a private place, the dom uses sunscreen to write obscene words, phrases, or doodles on the sub's skin, then allows them to become sunburned (either a little or a lot) so the invisible becomes visible! (Don't do this too often though—no need to get skin cancer for a little kinky fun.)

- The submissive is required to say a self-disparaging statement with every strike of an impact tool such as a whip or paddle.

- A damp, rolled up towel is used as a classic snapping tool of torment for a school-themed roleplay.

CHAPTER 18

ALL TIED UP WITH NOWHERE TO GO: BONDAGE, RESTRAINT, AND SENSORY DEPRIVATION

Being tied, blindfolded, gagged, and "abandoned" can also be very humiliating. So is urinary control, where sub isn't allowed to pee without permission. And being caged/ tied and "abandoned." In quotes because my domme has to remain in the apt/studio/house. Real abandonment is too dangerous to undertake.

- A

IF IMPACT PLAY IS ABOUT creating sensory overload, then bondage is about immobilization and deprivation of the senses, achieved through bindings, blindfolds, gags, etc. For many people who enjoy bondage outside of the humiliation context, this kind of play elicits a feeling of safety, connection, beauty, and comfort. The tools, as with impact play, are artful and used to make beautiful, symmetrical "presentations" of a submissive.

Not so in humiliation play. When bondage, restraint, and sensory depravation are employed in the name of erotic humiliation, it's all about creating situations that are ugly, absurd, and/or degrading. That's because, in the humiliation world, bondage explores the cultural contexts around ableism and what it means in our society to be denied power over our own bodies. While I cannot emphasize enough that there is *nothing* inherently shameful about being unable to use our bodies or our senses to their fullest potential, our society has taught us that physical disability robs us of our dignity. That absurd cultural context is what makes it good fodder for humiliation play.

Being purposely denied control of your physical body can trigger a deep feeling of embarrassment or humiliation due to the ableist cultural context that values mobility above all. Humiliation play eroticizes those feelings, and restricting movement or physical senses can be a powerful way to take control.

As with impact play, there are a variety of elements to consider when combining humiliation with bondage, including the materials, positions, predicaments, and body parts involved. We'll explore them all in this chapter, from head to toe. But first, I need to make a note about safety. This is not a bondage book—and I highly recommend you read one before you start exploring anything beyond the lightest bondage play—but because these activities, more than any others I talk about in this book, require a specific focus on physical safety, I can't talk about psychological bondage play without talking about how to do it while lowering the risk of physically injuring your partner.

Using sensory deprivation and bondage, or any kind of physical restraint, requires a high level of safety awareness. It's important to educate yourself on the specific safety skills needed for these activities through reputable books, online resources, and even in-person classes if those are available to you. Check the resource list at the back of this book for my recommendations, but here are a few basics to get you started, courtesy of my good friend Shay Tiziano at Bondag-eSafety.com:

- Disclose your health history before being tied up. Especially diabetes, asthma, joint issues, phobias/triggers, seizures, and nerve damage.

- Know signs of nerve damage, including (rapid onset) numbness, tingling, weakness, sharp shooting pains, or "bad pain." Submissives need to communicate if they're experiencing any of these things!

- Don't combine gags or any kind of breath play with bondage until the players have a strong familiarity with one another, and always have a safe signal that doesn't require words.

- Don't attach rope from the neck or genitals to a hard point

- Always monitor the person in bondage, and don't ever leave them unattended.

- Keep safety shears close by, and consider what would happen if the bottom fainted or fell, then adjust positioning, placement, and restraints as necessary to prevent serious injury or death should either occur.

HEAD

Okay now that you've read the safety basics—and, I hope, committed to researching bondage and restraint safety thoroughly before you try any of this on your own—let's dive in.

As I promised, we'll start at the top, the head. Hoods and blindfolds are an incredibly effective way of dehumanizing a submissive. These tools can be particularly helpful for folks who are new to humiliation play and/or partners that have a more egalitarian dynamic outside of kink play, because they allow players to more visibly "shift gears" and create some emotional distance. Pillowcases make excellent hoods, and since I'm known to be a bit silly at times, sometimes I like to draw a face on the fabric for an added laugh. (If silly faces aren't your cup of tea, that's okay. Pillowcases are equally effective—if slightly less amusing—without them.)

In contrast to the aesthetic nature of traditional bondage, humiliation fetishists tend to appreciate the humiliating experience of being made ugly or ridiculous. The rather uncomfortable nose hook, a device that hooks into both nostrils and pulls the nose up and back in a delightfully pig-like way, comes to mind as a popular example. You might have seen the DIY version of this device in the online "Scotch tape selfie" trend, where mainstream folks provided serious kinky inspiration by taping their faces into hilariously distorted, inhuman shapes. See? You don't need to spend a lot of money on equipment for humiliation-based bondage—all you need to turn a sub into a disfigured, mockable monster is a roll of tape. (Beware of messing with some people's hair though, as that can be a major limit for some folks, especially people of color.)

Another popular way to mess with a sub's head (literally and emotionally) is with a gag. There's a huge variety of gags available that are particularly perfect for humiliation play at a variety of levels of physical intensity. Players can experiment with everything from a bit gag (shaped like a horse's bit) that's made with a puppy teething toy (for the puppy play/bondage combo) to a piss funnel with a padlock (for fun with body fluids), to the an o-ring gag with exaggerated, bright red silicone lips, perfect for femmeslut-ifcation (a term I just invented to include bimboification, sissification, slut training, cross-dressing, or any other kink where bright red silicone lips might come in handy).

Note that, if you play with gags, you'll find out quickly whether you're a drool lover or not! Some people absolutely hate drool, even if they love gags. But the reality is that, when your mouth is stuffed or propped open, drool happens. It's just part of the reality of wearing gags, so you might have more fun if you just embrace it. Besides, think of the added embarrassment! A sub lying there, in whatever ridiculous position the dom has chosen for them, mouth filling with saliva until the wetness spills over their lips and down their chin, totally outside of their control, is humiliating, infantilizing, degrading, dehumanizing, and downright satisfying all rolled into one.

BODY BONDAGE

Just like with chastity or impact play, you don't need a lot of equipment to explore bondage and restraint. It can feel like there's an unspoken pressure in the kink world to do really intricate or heavy bondage, but I'm here to tell you that a pair of panties, a jockstrap, a leather belt, or even the oh-so-popular necktie wrapped around the wrists and/or ankles can be just as powerful (if not more so because of the symbology) as a full body of macrame rope or an expensive leather sleep sack. Be careful using pantyhose though, or anything that's too stretchy, because they can quickly cinch tightly enough to become an unintended tourniquet. If you're looking for ideas and inspiration for how to use clothing and other household items as bondage, I've listed a few fantastic resources in the back of this book.

My favorite form of low-impact, DIY, equipment-free bondage? Pulling a submissive's underwear down around their ankles and making them shuffle awkwardly around the room, like I did the first time I met wimpy.

> I met wimpy for the first time at a public dungeon play party. We had decided in advance to meet there for some impact play and already done our negotiations and everything. But first, I wanted to spend some time talking with my friends and settling into the party before turning my full attention to this new, never-been-destroyed (by me, at least) sub.
>
> In order to show him that I owned him and get him into the submissive mindset even before the scene, I told him I wanted him to play butler, bringing drinks and snacks for my friends and me while we were catching up. wimpy (still nameless at the time) was dressed very business casual— slacks, a polo, a belt—but I'd instructed him to

wear his nicest satin undies. So, I unbuckled his belt, opened up his pants, and pulled them down around his ankles, panties and all, so he could show them off as he shuffled back and forth from the bar with our drinks.

Public exposure combined with this light form of bondage—having wimpy hold up his shirt and shuffle around with his pants around the ankles— was so much more humiliating than just having him run around pantless, or even naked and cuffed. First, because it restricted his movement and made him look utterly ridiculous. Second, because there's a lot of vulnerable context to having your pants around your ankles: like someone walked in on you while you were peeing or before you'd finished getting dressed, or like you're a little kid being spanked or a drunken fraternity pledge getting paddled. Gotta love any activity that provides high levels of humiliation with very little effort or expense.

Plastic wrap, or cling film, can be another inexpensive way to explore bodily restriction, and it makes an excellent (and disposable) canvas for writing embarrassing, humiliating, or degrading words and phrases on someone's body (especially if you have any concerns about writing directly on skin). I love to wrap my subs' full torsos with their arms bound snugly at their sides, and then carefully rip the Plastic wrap or use safety shears to cut open areas around erogenous zones like nipples or genitals. Feeling the cool air on the exposed places, in contrast to the sweat accumulating under the wrap, can make for a heightened awareness of their most sexual and sensitive bits. Note that dehydration can be an issue with this kind of play, so keep water nearby, and don't forget the possible needs for bathroom breaks. You can even bring a plastic-wrapped submissive into a bathtub to rain down a golden shower on their freshly released (or still wrapped) body. And when you're all done, just ball up the plastic and throw it away—no need to worry about ruining your bondage materials!

Like I said, humiliation bondage is often very different from more traditional bondage. So if bondage is a core kink for the bottom, there are some devious ways to tap into common standards and turn fetishistic elements on their head. Using rope in a pretty way is often the goal of the bondage community, so to make it ugly, messy, or asymmetrical can be a particular torment for a bondage enthusiast. Many players also have personal preferences or rigid attitudes about the type of rope or material used for restraint. So someone who prefers a traditional Japanese approach (hemp rope, meticulous knots, symmetrical designs) might be delightfully anguished over the use of "lesser" materials (white nylon rope from the hardware store) and styles (messy, uneven knots or a haphazard design).

SMALL SPACES

When I'm feeling too impatient to use body bondage (which in my case is pretty often), I adore using small spaces to create the sense of physical restriction. For example, I would often tell my foot fetishist and objectification submissives that they were nothing different or better than the shoes I throw into the back of my closet, and then I would stick them in an

actual closet with the strict instructions to pleasure themselves (or not) while considering that reality.

Under the bed, or even the backseat of the car, are other
great places to stuff submissives.

> One time, a submissive client came over, and we
> were going to drive somewhere. I was in my twen-
> ties at the time, and my car was a bit of a mess, with
> food wrappers and other trash in the backseat. So
> I told the sub to crouch down in the footwells in
> the backseat of the car (which, in retrospect, was
> probably not super safe), and I told him to focus
> on the trash, embody the trash. I told him to really
> study those hamburger wrappers and understand
> that he was equal to them, that I was throwing him
> in the backseat like the trash that he was. Sounds
> harsh, but you know what? He loved it.

THE PERFECT POSITION

As I mentioned in the impact and sensation chapter, the
position a sub is stuck in (e.g., the back of the car) can be
just as powerful as the tools they're bound with. There are
some fantastic positions designed for exposure, discomfort,
and absurdity that we can take to the next level by adding
body bondage or furniture. Anything that spreads the body
wide and gives maximum access will do the trick, including a
St. Andrew's Cross, a spreader bar, or a restraint system used
to spread-eagle them on the bed. If you have the space, a
pillory (similar to stocks) is a historically accurate humiliation tool that's versatile enough to be used in scenes from
a vaudeville-inspired pie-in-the-face to a single-tail whipping and more. I had a submissive build one of these for my

professional dungeon for under $300, and it was a client favorite. (I will note, though, that a strong back is required to withstand bending over to be locked in the pillory, so this may not be good for a sub with back problems.)

If you have a particularly flexible submissive, you can use rope bondage to tie wrists to ankles, or ankles to thighs in a frog-tie position that's just as vulnerable as a spread-eagle. For someone with a cock and balls, a wooden humbler does exactly what it sounds like: It pulls the whole "private package" back tightly, which forces the individual to hunch over in a bowed position to avoid yanking their soft and squishy bits right off!

You can get similar effects with handcuffs as you can with rope bondage, but with the added benefit of even more humiliating context. Prisoner roleplay (whether we're talking old-school pillories or modern-day handcuffs) is based on how we dehumanize people in the prison-industrial complex—we see someone being in shackles as someone who is dangerous and doesn't deserve freedom. When we eroticize that, it makes for particularly humiliating play. (Separate from that cultural context, however, there are some interesting sensory aspects, including the sounds of clinking, the cold of the metal, and the weight of the cuffs and chains.) Metal handcuffs and shackles can be risky due to the focal pressure being on one tiny area with an unforgiving (and sharp) material, but they've always been a personal favorite of mine. Make sure that you have multiple, easy-to-access handcuff keys (that you double check actually work) before you lock someone up. Zip ties are hot in fantasy (and became even more popular after being mentioned in *50 Shades of Grey*), but they can cut into skin, and it can be tough to prevent them from continuously tightening.

BONDAGE AND SEXUAL PLAY

Bondage and restraint alone are a recipe for powerful humiliation play, but adding bondage to the more sexual play takes it to the next level by creating the concrete, physical feeling that the sub is being kept available and exposed. They're always ready for the dom to "use," and they can't prevent the sexual things that are going to happen (consensually, of course, even in a "forced" scene). Combining any level of restraint with the ideas in the "Coitus Humiliatus" chapter is likely to create some powerfully erotic scenes.

PREDICAMENTS

Oh, the sweet dilemma of having the keys to your own (erotic) destruction in your own hands! Predicament scenes, with the submissive "trapped" between two equally uncomfortable and/or demeaning options, are a wonderful way to combine bondage and humiliation. For example, I used to have a rotating stripper pole in my dungeon, and one time I plastic wrapped two submissives to either side at the same time and then whipped them all over their bodies. The predicament was whether each submissive wanted to be protective of the other and put *themselves* in harm's way, or would rather rotate away and "sell out" their predicament partner by forcing them to receive the blows.

> I really love predicament bondage and testing endurance. Forcing someone to fail at a predicament is so much fun, and if they succeed, the sense of satisfaction they get is nice too.
>
> - I

Another combination of humiliation, bondage, and sexual torment might be strapping a submissive into the humbler I mentioned before and then sitting on a counter and taunting them with the possibility of oral sex service so they have to stand up straighter (therefore pulling their sensitive bits tightly behind them) or miss out on such a delicious way to serve. Will they tolerate the discomfort to taste the sweetness of their dominant, or will they cave to the pain? Stay tuned to find out!

MORE WAYS TO PLAY

- The dom instructs the submissive to accomplish a difficult, routine, or ridiculous task while hindered by a spreader bar or "T-Rex arms tie."

- The dom uses a simple wrist tie to "control" a sub's hand while they masturbate, like a sex puppeteer.

- The sub wears asymmetrical bondage (rope, leather, or metal will work) to make movement awkward while dancing for or entertaining the dominant.

- A stainless steel anal hook with a rope body tie is used to add sexual stimulation or create a predicament scenario.

- The dominant puts the submissive in a sleep sack with purposefully placed zippers or creates a DIY bondage cocoon by tightly wrapping the submissive into an old sheet that's then cut (using safety scissors!) to create humiliating access points.

- The submissive's hands are locked into bondage mitts to deny them the use of their hands. Bonus points for doing this when they're incredibly horny and under orgasm control restrictions.

CHAPTER 19

EVERYONE IS WATCHING (BUT NOBODY CARES): PLAYING IN PUBLIC

A lot of times it's the people that are witnessing the act that make it more or less humiliating as opposed to the act itself. For example, being made to pee your pants in private is a little humiliating. Being made to do it in front of others much more so.

- ANONYMOUS

FOR LOTS OF HUMILIATION ENTHUSIASTS, having someone witness the experience either heightens the feelings of humiliation or is actually required for them to feel humiliated. Like a lot of humiliation play, if you want to take it public, there are different levels of exposure you can experiment with. For instance, there is a big difference between playing at a public dungeon or kink/BDSM event and going out into the "real world." Both allow you to be "seen" but with different levels of intensity and risk.

I'll admit that when I was younger and maybe more audacious, I was more flagrant in my public humiliation experiences. Back then, one of my favorite public humiliation activities was to trample subs in the middle of shoe stores on Boston's Newbury Street saying, "Oh, I think I could go hiking in these!" People would look away or at most mumble, "Weirdo," and then go back to their lunches and affairs and shopping lists. Those around us didn't care, but my submissives didn't realize this, and it only increased their humiliation. Here's another example:

> wimpy and I were in Las Vegas, which is like New York in that there is definitely more flexibility in people's expectation of weirdness. Again, I'm not talking about being obscene, but weird. wimpy had brought me and my best friend to Vegas to shop and see shows. Coming out of a show one evening, wimpy thought it would be funny to make a joke. I made a comment about wanting to get some exercise, and with a laugh, he said, "Yeah, you could use a little exercise, Princess." I stopped. He stopped. I said, "Okay...Let's think for a moment. Let's think for a moment about the words that just came out of your face." He had bought my girlfriend and me a bunch of clothes and souvenir goodies. He had been carrying all of the bags,

and I said, "You are going to take those bags and crawl through this casino. Then, we're going to get into a cab and you're going to crawl through our casino to get to our room." So, he got right down and crawled, trying to drag all of the bags along with him while awkwardly moving forward on his hands and knees.

I followed him while lightly kicking him in the ass, saying, "Yeah, who's fucking fat now? Yeah, who needs to exercise? You pig—let me hear you oink, pig. Who's a fucking piggy?" I was not shouting or anything, but I was rather stern and relentless. As I kicked him though the casino, a couple of security guys joined us. They didn't say anything since we weren't doing anything sexual; I wasn't causing a big scene, and wimpy was grinning like it was Christmas morning, so he was obviously not in any real harm.

When we started going through the second casino and got to the elevator, two women in their early twenties came up to us, giggled, and asked, "Is this sexual?"

I said, "Well, does it look sexual?"

One woman said, "I don't know."

Not wanting to spoil it, I thought quickly on my feet and responded, "Actually, I'm a trainer, and when men are inappropriate, their girlfriends or wives send them to me to gain compassion."

She was like, "That's genius."

"He had made a comment about his partner's weight, which was insensitive. What we're working through right now is the experience of being shamed in public."

I launched into this weird but reasonable-sounding explanation. Then, I kicked wimpy into the crowded elevator and said, "Okay, you can stand." One guy looked over at us and said, "It takes all kinds." He hit the door close button, and that was the end of the scene.

These days, I play it a little safer in terms of public humiliation. Forty-year-old Kali is less inclined to show off in the streets than twenty-year-old Kali was, but that doesn't mean it can't or shouldn't be a fun experience for other kinksters—though I will use this chapter to recommend certain precautions. Overall, most people are very wrapped up in themselves and their own lives, so the bottom line is that if you're not doing anything outright obscene, most people won't notice. Stay away from cops, and stop when you're around children and families (their parents have plenty of ways of screwing their own kids up without your help). Otherwise, people may glance, but they'll rarely say a word.

Going to kink events is a great way to start to explore being around other people in a safer environment, and there are many kinds to choose from: There are large BDSM events that take over whole hotels, fetish fairs where you can shop and network, classes, and other small, personalized kinky events. These are my personal preference for public play now, and they're what I enthusiastically recommend to others.

You can also go to places like porn shops. But please remember, just because they sell "obscene" materials, that does *not* give you an excuse to be obscene when you go there—it's just as rude as being obscene in a department store. They've seen it all, but it's still obnoxious to force others to be involved in your kinky scene. You don't want to be rude, and you don't want to be lewd—to people who haven't consented, anyhow. Be a discreet pervert, unlike I was in Amsterdam when I was in my late twenties or early thirties.

A submissive took me there on vacation, and he rented us separate rooms in a boutique hotel overlooking a square. Now, keep in mind that this particular sub was a rather tall, bulky, very hairy white man, then picture him in a pastel pink corset and garters, his hair bushing out of the top, with a mask obscuring his face. Once I got him all dolled up, I sat him in a window facing the square. I set him in profile and off to the side a bit so someone would have to be looking to see him. Still, he was hyperventilating about possibly being seen. Then, right in the middle of telling him nobody gave a shit about and nobody was looking at his lingerie, I looked down at the square to see a man looking up at the sub-slut, wearing the widest smile and giving us two thumbs up, completely delighted.

This isn't a fuck-up story. We had fun, and the guy loved what he saw, but it really could've gone the wrong way had someone with a different attitude seen the sub in that window above the square. I have no regrets since it turned out fine, but today, I wouldn't be so brash with public play, and I'd encourage you to be more discreet, too.

For somebody who's a foot fetishist, giving a foot rub in public can be an extremely embarrassing thing, first because the act itself turns them on and then because somebody might notice. The potential exposure is what pushes it over into delicious humiliation. I've taken my foot fetishist submissives to the park and teased them to give my feet "a little sniff. Just a little sniff. Just bend down..." and when they finally did, I'd say, "Oh, you *didn't!* Everybody was *looking*!" Ninety-nine times out of a hundred, nobody was looking. Regardless, being around other people who *might* see can be extremely exhilarating.

Another subtle way to engage in public play is through bondage worn under clothing. This is an excellent option anytime, anywhere. Using thin or thick rope, you can create a harness under your submissive's clothing that can be exposed for people to see or hidden to go unseen. Even if only your sub knows it's there, they will always be wondering if anyone is noticing. If it is obvious, then your submissive will receive curious stares and will feel embarrassed about letting people know.

As part of my safety protocols for professional domination sessions, I had potential playmates come and meet with me in a public spot—often a nearby McDonald's—so that I could approve them before inviting them to my dungeon. They always had to show up first, and they had to have a rose so that I could easily identify them. I'd show up, and they'd be sitting there with the roses, looking all nervous. I'd walk up and, in a casual voice, I'd say, "Hi, slut, how's it going?" They'd choke up and say, "Oh my god." I'd say, "Listen, nobody in here cares about you. Nobody heard me, because nobody cares." Just that experience of being called "slut" in public got their motors running in a way it never had before, as evidenced by their obvious expressions of horror and arousal. The power these actions have is rooted in the different contexts: The horror because this is not the way the outside world sees them, and the arousal because they were being publicly humiliated in a context that was ultimately safe. Again, this is something I probably wouldn't do today, this time because it wasn't explicitly consensual. But because of my skill, it was a safe environment, and it was very effective at the time.

I always grin when I'm doing mean things in public. People get very confused by that, which is the kind of confusion that I like!

EXTRA THINGS TO CONSIDER

Gender: The difference between being a dominant woman (or femme presenting) and a dominant man (or masculine presenting) is especially relevant in public humiliation. Women definitely have the upper hand in this type of situation, because women can do things to a man in public that, if a man did them so obviously, would be seen as abusive and would likely invite hostile looks and possibly interference from law enforcement. It is most important for male dominants with female submissives to keep things especially subtle so as not to attract too much unwanted attention.

Preparation: Scope out potential public play areas in advance if possible, or at least learn to do a quick but thorough look around before spontaneous play. Balancing possible exposure with privacy is the sweet spot we're looking for.

Safety: There's plenty of fun to be had without landing in jail and creating real problems in your life. Know what will get you in trouble, but in general follow these guidelines: no exposure, no genital contact or overtly sexual behavior (the law calls this "lewd and lascivious behavior"). Be especially aware of police and of any children and families around.

Practice: Prepare responses and drill them into your own head and your submissive's in case anyone in the public gets concerned. Practice different stories for different situations (e.g., it's a performance art piece, or they lost a bet).

Respect Vanilla Folks: It all depends on how you carry yourself, so be subtle; there's no need to be overly dramatic. If what you are doing is obviously disturbing a number of people, then tone it down a bit or go to another area to play. After all, discretion is sexy, and it's far less likely to get you arrested.

Many people don't believe that it's *ever* ethical to involve others in your scene without their explicit consent, and I agree with that. I don't *ever* condone treating strangers in a sexual way. Don't imagine that what you're doing is imperceptible or that it can't possibly affect people who don't know every detail of what's going on. Even an inkling of what's transpiring can make people feel put upon or used as props in a sexual game. Public humiliation is not about actively involving nonconsenting individuals in the sexual energy that you are both sharing.

PLACES TO PLAY

SHOPPING MALLS

Shoe stores and lingerie stores are great because you can have your submissive come out to model items or hold up sexy satin panties to their crotch on the sales floor to see if they'll fit. (Under no circumstances, though, is it appropriate to engage other customers or salespeople in your play. It's perfectly fine to hold up a thong to your submissive to see if it will fit, or even to ask clerks about sizing, pricing, and other questions you might ask in the course of a regular shopping trip, while letting the sub revel in the natural humiliation of the social experience. But it's not okay to engage in a way that uses a nonconsenting third party to ratchet up the intensity through active engagement, such as asking the salesperson or customer next to you if they agree that he'd look ridiculous in whatever you've picked out.)

At the mall, you can turn your submissive into an ATM by "withdrawing" money from their wallet (also see the chapter on Financial Domination), have the sub carry the shopping bags around like a donkey, or get your feet massaged surrounded by bags of purchases.

The food court is another great spot to play! When it's time for lunch, we sit down and take turns ordering. Since most of the food stands use disposable plates, there's no hygiene issue, so when it's time for the submissive to eat, I can spit right on the top of their food—say, three nice, big dollops of spit, then say, "Good boy. Now, go and eat." Again, if somebody was watching, they might be grossed out, but I would not have done anything illegal or sexualy obscene.

RESTAURANTS

Be respectful to your food server (always tip generously!), *never* use restaurant dishes for any kinds of bodily fluids, and always have a vanilla excuse prepared. With those caveats in mind, there are several ways to play publically in a restaurant: Send the submissive to the bathroom to silently masturbate or take off their panties, use a remote vibrator during dessert, or put cum in the salad dressing (using your own dishware or disposable takeout boxes—*never* dishes that waiters will have to touch or anyone else will have to eat off of, even after they've been washed).

PORN/SEX SHOPS

These are a good option for a taboo environment, but as I mentioned earlier, remember to be respectful of the employees. They've probably seen it all, but just like in the lingerie stores, it is not okay to involve them in your play. Also, be respectful of the other customers; some of them had to work up the courage just to go into the shop, and you might just scare them away forever. Go shopping together, and make the submissive bring all the toys up to the counter and pay for them. Or send the submissive in to collect a list of items you've already bought and paid for. Or have them go in to request the largest dildo available (or some other product they'll be embarrassed to ask for), but make sure you actually buy it and don't just waste the salesperson's time.

RENAISSANCE FAIRS

These are a great place to take your submissive; almost anything (legal) goes at these hedonistic affairs. Most people are carousing and don't take anything too seriously. If you brought your submissive on a leash and had them serve you as a king or queen, it would fit right into the spirit of the event. Dressing the part is part of the fun, so get as elaborate as you'd like. Most fairs have booths where you can rent a variety of costumes, from simple but appropriate to extravagant as royalty. People will be envious, and you'll draw a crowd for your antics. It might even be possible to sign the submissive up for a turn in the stocks to have food from the crowd flung at them. Or, if you'd rather keep it low-key, keep your actions subtler so no one notices. Play a part for the day—it may loosen up a side of yourself you've never seen before.

KINK/BDSM EVENTS

All over the United States, there are outdoor kinky camping events and hotel events that are excellent opportunities to explore erotic humiliation with a like-minded (and therefore the safest possible) audience. It is likely your public play will be met with appreciative glances from both fellow dominants and other green-eyed submissives on other people's leashes. It is also possible that there will be happenings at the event specifically designed to inspire humiliation play, such as themed parties or my popular "Erotic Humiliation Truth or Dare" games.

Let the public be your friend, your tool, and your respected ally. As long as you respect the fact that bystanders cannot give consent and avoid involving them unwillingly in your scenes, their unconcerned presence will add a delicious layer of risk to your humiliation play.

CHAPTER 20

WALKING WALLET$ AND HUMAN ATMS: FINANCIAL DOMINATION

Financial domination, begging my Goddess for the honor to pay further beyond my means. Also, when my Goddess decides that I am not worthy to see her on cam-session and she moves the camera so I pay to see darkness. I am not sure I have ever cum harder in my life than when I was paying $12 a minute and all I saw was darkness.

- FINANCIALPAYPIG

MONEY AND SEX ARE TWO of the biggest taboos out there, so if you combine them, you've got a whole buffet of taboos and triggers available to you to use for humiliation play.

The stories we grow up with, including those that reinforce our relationships to money, are not always clear to us. But one thing's for sure: Money is a powerful tool, and it can be a super-triggering thing for people. Kinksters can seem to have an extra layer of taboo around money. Many communities and individuals are adamantly against involving any kind of money play in kink, expressing a philosophy that keeping money out of the equation keeps the kink somehow "pure." This is nonsense. Money is incredibly powerful in our society, so taking control of someone's wallet renders them powerless and can create strong feelings of humiliation. Some people have a direct fetish for incorporating money. The financial part—far from sullying the "purity" of their experience—is essential for their arousal.

Financial domination is basically any technique of using money to dominate, arouse, control, and, for our purposes, to humiliate a partner. Money is a tool of power that can be used to great effect, but financial domination is not for everyone; use it if you are attracted to it, or ignore it and set it aside if you aren't. I've often said that financial domination (of any sort) is at one of the farthest edges of one of the edgiest ways to play.

Contrary to common belief, money kink doesn't have to include humiliation play. It can be explored as a respectful expression of affection or submission without any of the demeaning elements. That being said, thanks to the taboos around money that I mentioned earlier, it can be a source of abundant embarrassment play in all the right ways. What will determine the experience you have? Like usual, your own cultural context and your personal money stories will heavily influence the way you feel about incorporating finances (or not) into your fetishes.

We've talked about levels of play in humiliation, and about how you don't jump into the deep end if you haven't tested the water. The stereotype that "extreme" is the only speed at which to play with humiliation leads to the belief that all financial domination is at the "bankrupt or bust" level of engagement. This is simply not true. There are many opportunities to humiliate someone by controlling their wallet without the ultimately impractical humiliation of bankruptcy.

And then there are the gendered stereotypes that give financial domination a "bad name." The idea that all men who pay for things are sugar daddies and the idea that all women who enjoy being showered with gifts are gold diggers are both equally untrue.

Financial domination *can* be wielded like a great big sledgehammer, and there are certainly people out there who like to put themselves in real-world danger by putting their entire bank accounts on the line. The niche market of online financial domination is an example of this—it can have the feel of a dank, dark, dirty Las Vegas back room where everyone is betting big and losing hard. This can magnify some kinksters' already negative impressions of financial domination, as they only see the abusive "findom" creepsters online who are just looking for a payoff without any nuanced understanding of kink or of how a financial fetish works.

MONEY KINK'S BIGGEST OBSTACLE

One of the reasons financial domination has earned this shady reputation is that, more than any other type of kinky

players, findom enthusiasts have a tendency to resist negotiation. Let's be clear: Negotiation is possible. It's just that, for
financial players, the risk involved in going in without laying any groundwork is often part of the desire. In the same
way gamblers don't set boundaries with the dealer before
they ante up, financial submissives largely aren't interested
in negotiating with their dominants. Maybe the gambler
has a maximum number in mind, and maybe the sub does,
too, but when they get focused on the exhilaration of the
moment, those numbers quickly go out the window.

This is why we see some of the worst kink-related abuses in
financial domination play, because negotiation isn't part of
the equation. But that doesn't mean it can't or shouldn't be.
It can, and it must. It's just that, in money play, a little extra
psychological tap dancing is required to get that negotiation
going. Here are three tips to boost your odds:

- **Don't let language get in the way.** Many submissives have a negative association with the word
  "findom." If that's the case in your partnership, the
  solution is easy: Stop using that word. Just like in
  any kink, it's important to make the language (and
  tone of voice) work for you.

- **Don't be too direct.** Especially when you're
  warming up to constructive negotiation, direct
  questions like "What's your budget?" are likely to
  backfire. Instead, ask more slanted questions like,
  "What's the difference between your fantasy budget and your current financial situation?" or, "What
  do you have to sacrifice in your life to be able to
  tribute in this way?"

- **Make it a game.** Incorporate financial play into your negotiations by making subs pay for every question they respond to. Use a deck of cards (either one you make yourself or my "Pay to Play" card deck) to draw questions, determine prices, and wring information out of your subs in a way that's as fun as it is useful.

ETHICAL FINANCIAL DOMINATION

I love financial domination, and I fully believe it can be done ethically. As a result, I've become a specialist and something of an activist in this realm. I've been teaching specialized classes on the subject since 2014, including the popular virtual introductory classes and weekend intensives I started teaching in 2021 for sex workers about how to explore this kink with integrity. I've run into some negative responses in the kink community for it, and when lifestyle kinksters hear about my philosophy of ethical financial domination, their initial response is skeptical. I find it's a matter of perspective.

When they say, "Gosh, that's a lot of power to hold," I respond with, "I know. Like when you have somebody strung up and suspended and you've got a hundred clothespins on their body. I bet taking five bucks out of their wallet would really fuck them up, right?" Abuse of power is abuse of power. You can abuse your power regardless of what someone is willing to do for you—whether they put their genitals, their psyche, or their wallet in your hands.

It is just as possible to play ethically with money as with any other type of tool in kink. The key is communication, knowing and respecting boundaries, and finding out what you think is hot about it

As with any of these activities, submissives should be careful who they trust, how quickly they share personal information, and how much and how quickly they push their limits. Obviously you don't want to hand over your bank account info to someone you've had two coffee dates and one kink party adventure with (or worse yet, someone you've barely connected with online). Use common sense, and be responsible for your adult self.

MONEY KINK CATEGORIES

Erotic financial play is much more nuanced and personalizable that most people think. One of the elements you can consider when exploring it are the different money kink categories, which I define as pleasurable, painful, practical, and philosophical. Findom activities can occupy one or more of these categories at once, and understanding which categories are preferred can totally open up this type of play.

PLEASURABLE

This category is focused on making *both* the payer and the payee feel really good. It can be tributes focused on pampering, luxury, or nonessentials. Many kinksters who enjoy other fetishes such as latex, shoes, or bondage might be willing to spend money specifically on items that satisfy those desires, which would also fall under the pleasure category.

PAINFUL

This category is specifically about making the submissive who's spending feel the "pain." This can be about boundary pushing, punishing taxes, or the gamble and uncertainty of engagement games on social media.

PRACTICAL

This category is about the realistic financial needs in life. Anything from coffee and food delivery to bill paying to long-term investments. Approaching practical spending from an erotic perspective can help spice up a necessary part of life in lifestyle or personally commited relationships.

PHILOSOPHICAL

This category is about the fundamental belief that money can be used as a concrete form of power, and to hand it over is part of a value system, not just a kink. This can include chastity keyholding fees, reparations, and a "trickle up" tax from finsubs who believe their responsibility is to use their privilege to shower their dominants with gifts and other tributes.

PLAYING WITHIN YOUR MEANS

Besides the big, exceptionally dangerous fantasies around bankruptcy, there are plenty of ways you can play with money as a tool of humiliation in smaller, less destructive ways. My financial domination philosophy is, "I make 'reasonable' sexy." I put the focus on the power of money regardless of the level of spending. I emphasize that *any* control I exercise over their money is humiliating (for them).

It can be as simple (and practical) as buying a cup of coffee or purchasing groceries. Or perhaps something more pleasurable but still financially accessible, such as a pedicure or drinks out for you and a friend. The amount spent is not what's important, so wherever your financial boundaries are, that's okay. What's important is using money as an intentional erotic tool. And figuring out what style of control works for you and your partner.

> One of my favorite things to do with my submissives is pluck $20 out of their wallets to take a friend out for a drink. I'll make sure that I'm wearing something really tight or revealing, or maybe it'll be right after I get out of the shower. I'll lean down over their face as they kneel before me, I'll get right up close to their ear, and I'll whisper seductively, "Open your wallet." I'll say it really slow, and I'll stroke my body in a mesmerizing way. I'll command my submissive, "Open up your wallet so I can see that cold hard cash. Wider. Wider. I want you to spread that wallet wide open. Spread it open, bitch! Good, I want to see all the money. I want to play with it with my fingers. Mmm, do you mind if I stroke your money for a second?"

See what a different feeling that is than to say diffidently, "Hey, human ATM, go get me some more money, because that's all you're good for." It can be sensual. It can be dismissive. It can be more about the control than the cash.

Being a human ATM, of course, is very fun for some. I had a personal submissive who served me well for quite a few years. When we first met, he asked if he could buy me a pair of designer shoes, though he didn't realize what he was getting himself into when he did! I was immediately hooked—shoes have always been a weakness of mine, and I learned quickly that stylish, well-crafted shoes were an excellent investment (by him, of course).

He had gotten me completely addicted to designer shoes, so every time I would go out to visit him, I'd say, "Let's go to the mall! Time to adorn My glorious feet!" We would go to all the different stores, and we'd load him down with bags. Every time we'd go to a shop, I'd say, "Credit card. Money. Money for me. Give me your credit card." How humiliating was it for him to just hand it over and say, "How much?" I'd say, "It doesn't matter. Give me the card."

You can use that to your own levels and combine it with other forms of play—with sissification, for example, you can say, "I'm going to buy you ten pairs of panties, and it's coming out of your allowance." If you're in a personal relationship, there are ways to do it without putting you both into bankruptcy.

> On an especially exhibitionistic excursion to Victoria's Secret with wimpy, I had loaded him down with bags and bags and bags from all of the shopping we were doing. He walked around the store with me, and in addition to the bags he was carrying, I kept hanging all of the bras and panties off of his pockets and pants. The salesgirls kept coming up to ask, "Do you want me to take those bags?" I kept having to say, "No, no, no. He's happy as can be. Don't worry about him. He's my little shopping donkey. He's got all the bags."

You'd be surprised at how aware people are about this sort of thing (especially now that there's been some mainstream coverage of the kink—even the *New York Times* did an article on it!). They may not completely understand the dynamics of what we're doing, but they understand that there are people like us in the world. You don't have to hit them over the head with it, and in fact you shouldn't.

> *I have a submissive who enjoyed very subtle public play, we called them Domme Dinners, where I would order for him, speak over him, demand his credit card (loudly) or be like, "Oh no honey, he doesn't get the bill." and then pay with a card with his name on it, etc. It was super fun!*
>
> *- Vela Verres*

Money kink is especially perfect for play that centers around games, predicaments, and betting. For example, rolling the dice to determine how much the tribute will be.

In a completely different way of using financial domination, you can flip it on its head and use the idea of a submissive *accepting* money as a humiliating act. It's not a technique that would generally leap to mind when most people think of financial domination, but it can be just as useful. Some submissives have deeply embedded pride issues around supporting themselves financially. If these submissives are put in a (real or imagined) dire financial situation, or even if they're just in momentary need of financial help, then you might as well eroticize that experience of "forcing" them to accept the financial assistance that a dominant is offering.

Another way to exert financial domination is through budgeting and allowances. Does the submissive struggle with sticking to a budget? For a bonus twofer, incorporate kinky play into building better life habits. Is impulse shopping an issue? Require that the submissive beg and plead and make their case before granting (or not granting) permission to spend their own money.

USING YOUR SENSES WHEN PLAYING WITH DOLLARS

Both paper and coin money can be explored through physical sense, which can make for an erotic session even when budgeting doesn't allow for real money to be exchanged. Listen to the crinkle of a one (or twenty, or hundred) dollar bill and the clinking of coins falling through fingertips. The beeping of an ATM and the whoosh of cash as it dispenses *your* money into *my* hands. Think of sex scenes with sweaty bodies rolling over slippery bills covering a bed.

Financial domination tends to have a lot of particular baggage and taboo; it's very important that you negotiate around these actions before putting them into use. It is very possible to play with money both erotically and ethically, but it requires communication of where boundaries are, along with respect of those boundaries.

In many ways, financial domination is the edgiest of edgy ways to play. But like all kink, there is a wide variety of styles, levels, intentions you can play with to create the perfect amount of risk to get you off without ruining your life. It is possible; please seek it!

MORE WAYS TO PLAY

- The dom sets up a direct deposit from the submissive's account to an IRA to save for their future.

- Every month at an appointed time, the sub is required to present cash to pay for a specific bill.

- The dom chooses a luxury the submissive can forgo to pay for a luxury the dominant wants.

- Behavior modification techniques are used to train the submissive to use a budget.

- The submissive goes through trash to collect recycling to trade in for cash to spend.

- A foot fetishist places a dollar at their dom's feet every time they kiss one of their toes.

- The dom goes shopping with the submissive and has them highlight their favorite purchases on the receipt.

- After going shopping, the sub is allowed to kiss their favorite body part once for every $10 they've spent.

- Once a week or month, the sub is instructed to purchase a book off the dominant's Amazon wish list.

- In a cuckolding scenario, the submissive is required to pay for a date with the dominant and their lover.

CONCLUSION

WHEW, THAT'S QUITE A TOUR through the wide, wonderful world of erotic humiliation! The huge variety in activities and approaches is one of the reasons I am continually drawn to playing with this psychologically potent kink. One of the most common comments I hear when I teach this topic live is that a kinkster has come to the class "just to check it out," believing that they don't have an interest in erotic humiliation. After listening to me talk, and to others in the class share their fantasies and experiences, they discover that they've *already* experienced this type of play (or have a desire for it) but simply have never thought of it as humiliation since it didn't make them feel "bad" (one of those common stereotypes I talked about at the start of the book).

Like all of the other taboo activities that comprise kinky behavior, the end goal should always be a feeling of positivity and arousal. As you digest the information you've read in this book and start incorporating it into your play — or planning to do so in the future—take these final reminders to heart to ensure you're creating safe, mutually satisfying scenes for you and your partner:

You can't humiliate someone with something they don't find humiliating, so this kind of kinky play is all about getting to know your partner and sharing the things that get you going.

Communication, as in all kink play, is high-priority. So even if it's challenging to express your desires, fantasies, and limits, *find a way.* Words are powerful, both as a way to share what your interests are and to engage the brain during scenes.

Take the time to negotiate, not only the activities and actions, but the kernel kinks (goal feelings) for everyone involved. There are as many ways to experience erotic humiliation as there are humans on earth, which makes it personal and nuanced. So spending time figuring out what you want and how you want it is an important way to set yourselves up for successful experiences.

And finally, remember that this is play! Adding kinky theatrics to sex can be fun and even productive. Explore and adventure to your heart's content, always prioritizing these five important components: Consent, Context, Intention, Trust, and Communication.

Visit EnoughToMakeYouBlush.com for more support for your erotic humliiation journey, including additional blog posts, links, videos, community resources, and ongoing surveys where you can share your experiences and possibly be quoted in a future edition or other titles.

Now, go forth and enjoy the BLUSH!

GLOSSARY

Active Ignoring—A phrase I've coined to describe my recommended way to do abandonment play, which includes acknowledgment during the ignoring.

Aftercare—Any sort of "closure" done after a scene. For example, having snuggle time or discussing how the scene went.

BDSM—A popular acronym for Bondage/Discipline, Dominance/Submission, SadoMasochism.

The Bubble—A phrase I've coined to describe the "safe space" of erotically charged activities that still retain the "real world" context.

Chastity—The denial of orgasm, but even more specifically the control of orgasm.

Cis-Het—A shortened version of the term "Cisgender Heterosexual," referring to someone who identifies with the gender they were assigned at birth and is attracted to the opposite sex.

Consensual—A quality of interaction based on explicit, informed, and enthusiastic agreement to and desire for the action at hand.

Consensual Non-consent—A scene that contains an element of "force" that has been pre-negotiated.

Cuckolding—An informed and consenting arrangement of infidelity enacted for the titillation of the passive partner. It can also be called "cuckqueaning" when the submissive is female.

Edging—A pattern of masturbating right up until you're ready to cum and then stopping and letting the build-up die away.

Erotic Slut Shaming—A type of humiliation play that centralizes the erotic body and arousal as the target of torment

Fetish – A form of sexual desire in which gratification is linked *to an abnormal degree* to a particular object, item of clothing, part of the body, etc.

Figging—Using a peeled piece of ginger carved into the shape of a butt-plug as a form of anal "torture." The spiciness of the ginger causes a burning sensation inside the anus.

Financial Domination—Any technique of using money to dominate.

Fluid Bonded—Players who have exchanged bodily fluids with one another, such as by having penetrative sex without a condom or oral sex without a dental dam.

Hot Button—See Trigger

Humiliatrix—A term some female-identified dominants use to describe themselves.

Intensity—The level or degree to which the submissive partner is humiliated within a scene. These degrees range from embarrassment (the lightest intensity) to degradation (the heaviest).

Kali's Teeth—A device with spikes that can be added to a chastity cage.

Kernel Kink—A phrase I use to describe the core aspect of your kink, the *why* rather than the *how*, the feeling desired rather than the action taken.

Kink—A strong sexual attraction to nontraditional interests. A kink is a taste or a preference, but it's a "nice to have," not a "must have."

Kink Extravaganza—A phrase I've coined to describe the perceived need to have elaborate, complex scenes every time you play.

Munch—A social gathering, typically defined by a theme (age players, new to the scene, city-specific, etc.), that tends to be more of a casual get-together where kinky people can meet in a vanilla/non-kinky environment.

Non-consent—The absence of explicit, informed, and enthusiastic agreement to proceed.

Pavlov Yourself—A phrase I've coined, derived from the experiments of Dr. Ivan Pavlov, to describe the act of ritualizing and using behavior training to achieve a certain feeling or headspace.

Pickup Play—When two or more people meet at a dungeon, munch, or other social play venue and play without knowing each other beforehand.

Praise Kink—A form of erotic humiliation play in which the dominant requires the submissive to stand in front of them and receive sincere compliments until they're so overwhelmed and embarrassed they can't stand it.

P.R.I.C.K.—Personal Responsibility in Consensual Kink is the only framework that specifically advocates for both parties (yes, subs, too) to take an *active* role in advocating and managing consent.

Protocol—Rules for how certain things should be done, such as how a submissive should stand or how they should speak when spoken to.

R.A.C.K.—Risk Aware Consensual Kink is a safety motto that serves as a reminder to stay aware of the risks, both physical and psychological, that come with any level of not just kink, but any sexual interaction.

Ramping Up—A phrase to describe the most effective way to play with intensity, not making sudden jumps but steadily increasing so that it's easy to stop at discovered limits.

Ruined Orgasm—When someone gets to the point of cumming and something is done to ruin it.

SSC—"Safe, Sane, and Consensual" was traditionally the most popular motto used to characterize careful kink, though it's beginning to be replaced by others such as R.A.C.K. and P.R.I.C.K.

Safeword—A coded word or phrase used to bring a halt to the action, typically an unusual word that has no ambiguous interpretation.

Sensory Sparks—A phrase I've coined to describe a strategy to kickstart a desired mindset or feeling by associating it with a particular smell, taste, feel, object, or word, using sense memory to spark the target emotional state.

Shortcut—A communication tool (such as a safeword) that uses a single word or short phrase to convey a larger concept.

Stage Whispers—A phrase I use to describe the sort of behind-the-scenes communication that might need to take place *during* a scene.

Sub Space and Top Space—A state of mind and set of default understandings that define and outline an individual's role and expectations in a scene.

Sub Drop and Top Drop—The sudden physiological circumstance that results from the removal of stimuli and the cessation of a scene, typically requiring aftercare.

The Scene—Some BDSM community members may refer to the entire kink community as "The Scene."

A scene—When the word "scene" has a lowercase "s," it usually references the time frame when kinky people are playing (a.k.a. a session).

Style—The different tones and roles a humiliation scene can incorporate based on players' desires, including but not limited to sensual, authoritative, mocking, and cruel.

Topping from the Bottom—The concept that a submissive is attempting to control the dynamic or scene by sharing their desires.

Trigger (see also "Hot Button")—A word/phrase/action that elicits a strong negative response.

Trigger Plan—A predetermined and negotiated plan for how to care for either player when a trigger or hot button is tripped in a scene.

Truism—A statement made to imply or assert that there is only "one true way" to approach any aspect of play in the kink community when, in reality, there is no single path to "real" kink expression.

Vanilla—A term some people use in the BDSM community to indicate someone or something that is non-kinky.

SUGGESTED ONLINE RESOURCES

KinkAcademy.com—This is a website I created in 2007 that now features over 2,000 videos by over 150 educators (myself included). It's a huge resource where you can learn from watching, pausing, rewinding, and watching again. There's a variety of expert perspectives represented, and these are some of the series that I'd recommend based on subjects I covered in this book:

- "Clothing Bondage" by Lee Harrington
- "Advanced Negotiation" by Thista Minai
- "Cigar Play" by Naiia and Strangerfriend
- "Boundary Smackdown" by Mollena Williams
- "Embarrass, Humiliate, Degrade, Objectify" by Nayland

CoachingByKali.com—I offer personal coaching sessions to lifestyle and professional kinksters, most frequently focusing on dominant and submissive dynamics, specific relationship obstacles, and new ways to play and explore. Singles, couples and poly groups are all welcome, as well as anyone anywhere along the gender spectrum.

BondageSafety.com—Shay and Stefanos Tiziano are two of my personal favorite educators, and since Shay is a medical professional with a penchant for deep, detailed knowledge, they're certainly a bondage resource you can trust.

SubmissiveGuide.com and **DominantGuide.com**—Two websites that offer extensive, high quality information for submissives and dominants respectively. They offer articles, ebooks, ecourses and so much more. I'm a big fan!

Fetlife.com—A social site for kinksters. It's a great way to find events near you and connect with others who share your interests (though it's not structured as a dating site). There's a large number of "groups" based on various activities and affiliations and it can be a good place to find information and inspiration. However, I caution you to be careful who you listen to since there's zero vetting happening on that site.

NSCFreedom.org's KAP List (Kink-Aware Professionals)—A "listing of psychotherapeutic, medical, legal and other professionals who have stated that they are knowledgeable about and sensitive to diverse expressions of sexuality."

ScottPaulDesigns.com—The creator of the "Humiliator Gag System," an innovative and incredibly versatile item that can be useful in many types of scenes. You can purchase a serving tray, toilet brush, feather duster, ash tray, boot brush, dildo, and toilet paper dispenser—all of which click interchangeably into the mouth gag piece.

Stockroom.com—This site sells a huge selection of sex toys and BDSM gear. You can find just about anything you fantasize about here, including many items I mentioned throughout the book, such as the forced watersports gag, dildo gag, chastity devices, bondage needs, and so much more.

Etsy.com—It might surprise you that this virtual marketplace has quite the bustling kink niche. Everything from novelty print T-shirts and underwear to handmade impact and sensation toys to full-size dungeon furniture pieces. Just search using your favorite kinky words, and see what wonders turn up!

RECOMMENDED READING

- *Exhibitionism for the Shy: Show Off, Dress Up and Talk Hot!* by Carol Queen
- *Tying and Flying: Bondage for Self-Suspension* by Shay Tiziano and Stefanos Tiziano
- *Better Bondage for Every Body: With Rope Bondage Experts from Around the World* by Evie Vane
- *The Forked Tongue Revisited: A Handbook for Treating People Badly* by Flagg
- *The Toybag Guide to Playing With Taboo* by Mollena Williams
- *The Toybag Guide to Age Play* by Lee Harrington
- *My Gender Workbook* by Kate Bornstein
- *The Lazy Crossdresser* by Charles Anders

ABOUT THE AUTHOR

ONE OF THE KINK COMMUNITY'S premier speakers and entrepreneurs, Princess Kali is the founder of KinkAcademy.com, a revolutionary online sex and kink education resource for erotic adventurers, and of the Red Key Club, a business and marketing school for sex workers. She is also the author of ten books and workbooks including *Enough to Make You Blush: Exploring Erotic Humiliation*. For twenty years, Kali has been deeply engaged in exploring the whys and hows of erotic humiliation and other misunderstood forms of kink play. Kali is a member of the CARAS Research Advisory Committee and in 2022 was inducted into the Dominatrix Hall of Fame. With an international reputation among lifestyle and professional kinksters, she has dedicated her life to creating unique educational tools, workshops, and retreats to help consenting and creative adults explore sexual expression safely.

ACKNOWLEDGEMENTS

I'VE SAID FOR MANY YEARS, "It takes a village to support this Princess!" and that was true for this book as well.

I want to thank Brian Flaherty and Meg Elison for all of their assistance with editing the original edition. Not only did you help corral my words and hone my voice, but you improved the book in so many ways.

I'm extremely thankful to Sarah Welch, my powerhouse editor, for not only being a total pleasure to work with but also for being so adept at working with my rather unorthodox material. How did I ever get any writing projects done without you?! You have leveled up every word I publish, and I quite honestly can't thank you enough.

My sincerest thanks to Sarah Mason, who did all the class transcriptions for the first edition. I regretfully overlooked including her in the original acknowledgements. Your work was pivotal to getting enough words on the page to turn those pages into a book. Thank you for listening to hours and hours of my thoughts on this subject and for such meticulous skill in transcription!

My deep gratitude goes to Megara for her brilliant use of post-it notes, and years of encouragement, brainstorming, and support, both professionally and personally. I'm so thankful for your friendship.

I cannot begin to express my thanks to Sinclair Sexsmith, a truly stellar friend and fellow kink philosopher, for the many, *many* hours of meandering and intentional conversations before, during, and after the updated writing of this book.

Special thanks to Marcia Baczynski, the third member of the Three Tops Club (along with Sinclair and me) for fabulous feedback and on-going support!

I would also like to extend my gratitude to the brilliant educators and friends I had the pleasure of speaking with for the new chapters. Lucie Fielding, you're doing such important work and are truly such a delight! Shay Tiziano, the kink world is so wildly lucky to have you. Thanks for all you do.

Big thanks go to Nicole Mazzeo for wearing so many hats—from social media management to graphic design and beyond—and supporting me in so many ways, both on this book and my work in general, and for being a joy to work with.

My ongoing appreciation also goes to Hannah Portello-Swagel for all of the excellent design work on the entire *Blush* line of books and decks. After so many years working together, I continue to be grateful. Thank you for working your "Hannah magic" to take my design ideas and make them sparkle.

Thanks also to Alex Head from The Draft Lab for the fast and responsive work formatting this book on a tight turnaround. I'm delighted with how it turned out!

A very special and heartfelt thanks goes to all of my current and past submissives, without whom I wouldn't be the dominant I am today. I thank them for all of the opportunities to play, practice, and learn and for their years of devoted service.

I am indebted to everyone who has shared their experiences with me—those that have taken the time to comment on my surveys and come to my classes over the past two decades and more. The kinksters I have met in the BDSM community keep me curious, entertained, and even after two decades, always coming back for more!

WORK WITH KALI

DEEPER SHADE OF RED:
VIRTUAL INTENSIVE

Stop shying away from erotic humiliation play because you don't feel skilled enough to handle it. Exploring erotic humiliation is such a personal experience, but this fully immersive and interactive workshop will give you the guidance you need to begin—or further—your journey.

Erotic humiliation is a state of mind that can be cultivated through a huge variety of types of activities. Not only will the weekend include an in-depth explanation of the overall mechanics of psychological play, but we'll also go into detail about specific types of scenes and how to make them work for you. We'll spend time exploring your interests, goals, and motivations to get to the heart of creating the experiences you're craving.

www.DeeperShadeOfRed.com

ETHICAL FINANCIAL DOMINATION:
VIRTUAL INTENSIVE

Financial fetish is one of the most misunderstood power play experiences, even by those who practice it. With this two-day fully immersive workshop, you'll turn doubt and confusion into confidence and clarity when it comes to incorporating money-kink into your unique brand in a way that appeals to your best-matched clients.

Discover a deeper understanding of the intersection of money, kink, and control. Transform your professional approach to financial domination with personalized insight, an environment of encouragement and support, and the opportunity to develop an authentic, ethical approach to exploring financial fetish.

This event is designed for ProDommes, Cam Models, Phone Sex Operators, and other erotic professionals only.

www.EthicalFinancialDomination.com

JOIN ME AT A CLASS, INTENSIVE, OR COACHING SESSION

Would you like to work with me directly? I offer one-on-one and group coaching programs as well as in-person retreats throughout the year. Find more information at

www.CoachingByKali.com

All coaching sessions are done over video or phone call, and I work with both lifestyle and professional players.

If you have any questions, feel free to email me directly at

ThePrincessKali@Gmail.com

FOLLOW ME ON SOCIAL MEDIA

Twitter: @ThePrincessKali
Instagram: @ThePrincessKali
Fetlife: @ThePrincessKali

LEAVE A REVIEW ON AMAZON OR ETSY

Reviews are one of the most helpful things for an author, so if you enjoyed the book, please leave a review wherever you purchased the book. You can also review it on Goodreads!

Printed in Great Britain
by Amazon

22106817R00190